fried & true

fried & true

**Crispy and Delicious Dishes
from Appetizers to Desserts**

Rick Rodgers

Photographs by Christopher Hirsheimer

CHRONICLE BOOKS
SAN FRANCISCO

Library of Congress Cataloging-in-Publication Data:

Rodgers, Rick, 1953–
    Fried and true: crispy and delicious dishes from appetizers to desserts/
    by Rick Rodgers; photographs by Christopher Hirsheimer.
    144 p.   22.2 x 20.4 cm.
    Includes index.
    ISBN 0-8118-1606-0 (pbk.)
    1. Deep frying. 2. Cookery, International. I. Title.

  TX689.R62 1999
  641.7'7—dc21   98-13202
                                                                CIP

Manufactured in China.

Design: Yumiko Nakagawa
Food styling: Melissa Hamilton
Kitchen assistant: Budd Connelly

Distributed in Canada by Raincoast Books
9050 Shaughnessy Street
Vancouver, British Columbia V6P 6E5

10 9 8 7 6

Chronicle Books LLC
85 Second Street
San Francisco, California 94105

www.chroniclebooks.com

Acknowledgments

There is only one name listed as author of this book, but in reality, there are many people who contributed to the book you now see.

First, I want to thank Bill LeBlond of Chronicle Books. Bill and I were nibbling at dishes of deep-fried artichokes and golden calamari when we agreed that deep-frying should have a cookbook that treated it with the respect it deserves. Sarah Putman picked up the ball and edited the book with aplomb. Christopher Hirsheimer provided photographs that caught every crunch and crackle, and the food stylist, Melissa Hamilton, perfectly captured the spirit of the recipes. Thanks to Yumiko Nakagawa, whose elegant design of the book makes it a pleasure to look at. And special thanks to copy editor Carolyn Miller for improving my prose.

I am always thankful for my friendship with Diane Kniss and Steven Evasew, with whom I have shared recipes and good times for many years. And to Patrick Fisher, who didn't complain (who would?) after weeks of deep-fried dinners. I am also grateful to Richard Braun and T-Fal, for providing their excellent deep-fryer for recipe testing.

contents

frittering away

Crispy, golden brown potato chips. Spicy Buffalo chicken wings dipped into blue cheese sauce. Tender zucchini blossoms in a delicate white wine batter. Still-warm buttermilk doughnuts with an apple cider glaze.

Is your mouth watering? I'll bet it is. It's no surprise that all of these appetite-teasing foods are deep-fried, a cooking technique that may be battered (pun intended) by the food police, but one that will never be abandoned by good cooks. The steak is back, martinis are back, fondue is back, cigars are back, and deep-fried foods never left. I'll admit that more restaurants are serving grilled boneless, skinless chicken breasts than ten years ago, but they are also serving more calamari, Buffalo wings, zucchini sticks, mozzarella sticks, sweet potato fries, chimichangas, and countless other deep-fried goodies. Chefs are topping their mashed potatoes with frizzled shallots, garnishing their polenta with deep-fried sage leaves, and shoveling up tons of tortilla chips. Why? Because people love fried food! Studies have shown that hearing and touch, along with the other more obvious senses like taste and smell, also come into play when we eat, and humans find crunchy sounds and crispy textures irresistible. ("Snap, Crackle, and Pop" to you, too!)

There is room for deep-frying in a healthy life style. A good diet is *balanced*. Unfortunately, too many Americans eat too much fat every day, and don't save special foods for special occasions. (Most of us tend to forget that real exercise is more exerting than getting up from the La-Z-Boy chair to get another snack.) Deep-fried foods are for the times in your life when you want to indulge, celebrate, and have fun. I am not saying deep-fried foods should be everyday fare. But when you do succumb to the temptation of perfectly fried chicken or Grandma's recipe for fried Christmas cookies, they should be wonderful. (It's interesting to note that many old-country holiday recipes, especially those of the Mediterranean, are deep-fried. While households may not have had ovens, they had a stove, a pot, and lots of olive oil.) Some of the recipes in this book could be enjoyed for a weeknight supper, but most of them are most at home in a party setting.

Done correctly, deep-frying creates a delectable crisp coating that just can't be duplicated by other cooking methods. With a couple of exceptions, I have chosen to concentrate on deep-frying, not panfrying or stir-frying. But deep-frying isn't a common home cooking technique like broiling or sautéing, and people forget the basic rules and start practically from square one every time, forgetting what they may have learned the last time they deep-fried. Cooking in hot oil is really no more complicated than cooking in boiling water. Some foods cook better in simmering water; others cook better in boiling water. It's the same with hot fat: Keep it at the proper temperature, and the food will cook beautifully.

Fried & True will show you how to make perfect deep-fried food every time. So get out the deep fryer and get ready to make something delicious!

Deep-Frying Basics

Of all the major cooking techniques, deep-frying is the one that cooks understand least. The premise is simple. Food, usually battered (to keep the food's surface moisture from coming in contact with the hot oil, which would cause splattering), is added to a pot of hot fat. The fat immediately surrounds the food and cooks it from all sides, creating an exterior layer that seals the food's flavors and juices inside. The fat temperature determines how long the food will take to cook through on the inside and become golden and crisp on the outside. Properly prepared, deep-fried foods absorb much less fat than you would expect. If you choose the right pot and the right fat, and set yourself up with a couple of utensils, deep-frying is a quick, fun, and delicious way to cook.

Utensil Central

There are many different deep fryers available, from fancy electric models to tried-and-true standbys like woks and cast-iron Dutch ovens. They all work, but some are better suited for certain jobs than others. There are two issues to consider when choosing a deep fryer: the pot's capacity and its ability to hold heat well.

The fryer should be at least 6 inches deep, allowing it to be filled one third to halfway full with 2 to 3 inches of fat so that the food can literally swim in it. "Deep" frying, get it? Food will fry best and absorb less fat if it is completely immersed. One of the most common deep-frying mistakes occurs when the cook doesn't use enough fat. Don't fill the pot more than halfway full, however, to allow for the inevitable bubbling that

occurs when food is added. I estimate 3 pounds of shortening or $2\frac{1}{2}$ quarts of oil for most frying jobs. Some foods, by contrast, are best cooked in a skillet, which should be at least 2 to 3 inches deep—enough to hold at least 1 inch of fat. Both deep fryers and skillets should be large; if food is crowded in a too-small utensil, the food will give off too much steam and end up soggy, not crisp.

When the fat reaches its proper temperature, the food is added, which makes the fat temperature drop. Thus the pot should be heavy and made of a thick metal that absorbs and holds heat and allows the temperature to rise again. If the fryer is electric, it should have enough wattage to drive the temperature back up. Following are some of the various containers for frying:

Electric Deep Fryers: Electric deep fryers are great for the cook who deep-fries fairly often. Their biggest attraction is a special filter that soaks up deep-frying odors (some of the filters are easier to remove than others, so check out this feature out before buying). One manufacturer has a basket that rotates in and out of the oil, an action that supposedly cuts down on oil absorption. Some have windows in their lids to allow the cook to see the cooking food (although I find that the steam released during cooking clouds up the windows). Deep fryers with nonstick interiors are easiest to clean, but be sure they don't have any hidden nooks and crannies, or as soon as you add fat, the crumbs hiding in the crevices will come floating to the top.

Keep in mind that most electric fryers have a relatively small capacity. They work best for bite-sized foods such as hors d'oeuvres, shrimp, and cookies. Most models would be hard-pressed to deep-fry an entire chicken. As for power, choose a fryer with the highest wattage possible to allow for the quickest heating of the fat and the fastest temperature recovery after food has been added. On the other hand, if you have older electrical wiring where you live, you may want a lower-wattage fryer, so you don't overload your circuit breaker if you are sharing the outlet with another appliance.

Electric Multi-Cookers: Multi-cookers have adjustable electric thermostats that allow the pot to be used for a variety of cooking methods. While I originally bought my multicooker to use as a slow cooker (it also braises, simmers, and boils), I use it most often as a deep fryer. Multi-cookers are less bulky than electric deep fryers, but they do not have the odor-absorbing filters that are so useful.

Woks: Deep-frying is important in Asian cuisine. What would Chinese food be without its egg rolls, wontons, and other crispy treats? Woks make excellent deep fryers. They have a wide, deep cooking area that allows oil to heat up quickly, and the shape encourages heat to travel up the sides and stabilize the oil temperature. For deep-frying, be sure to use a flat-bottomed wok, not a rounded one that sits on a ring. The flat-bottomed wok is more stable and comes in better contact with the heat source to maintain the fat's temperature. Most Chinese cooks recommend that the wok be heated until very hot before adding oil, believing that the oil heats more quickly when added to a hot pan. It is hard to use a deep-frying thermometer with a wok; instead you may need to check the temperature of the fat with a cube of bread or chopsticks (see "Setting Up," below). While I do not like electric woks for stir-frying because they don't get as hot as stove-top models, they make fine deep fryers.

Skillets: Some thin foods can be deep-fried in 1 inch of hot fat in a skillet. The skillet must be at least 2 or 3 inches deep. Cast-iron skillets are preferred, as they hold heat best. Never wash a cast-iron skillet with soap and water—just sprinkle the inside with a handful of coarse salt, and wipe it out with wads of paper towels. Electric skillets aren't good deep fryers, as they just aren't deep enough.

Dutch Ovens: My favorite deep-frying pot is a 5-quart enameled cast-iron Dutch oven. It holds a 3-pound can of melted vegetable shortening to make a deep pool for frying food properly, heats up quickly over high heat, and keeps fat at the desired temperature, thanks to its thick, heat-absorbent walls. Uncoated cast-iron pots also work well. If you don't have cast iron, use a heavy pot with a minimum 4-quart capacity. Anything smaller will crowd the food and lead to soggy disaster.

The Right Oil

To some cooks, devoted to a low-fat diet, there will never be a "right" fat. Yet fat is an essential nutrient, along with protein and carbohydrates, and shouldn't be removed completely from our diet, though of course it also shouldn't be consumed to excess. Most people would be better off if they substituted the daily bag of chips with their sandwich with pretzels or an apple, the better to indulge in sensational homemade potato chips at their next party. Also, at home, you are in control of the kind of fat you use. If you don't indulge in deep-fried foods on a regular basis, use the fat that gives the best results for the food being cooked. In the recipes in this book, you can use whatever fat you prefer, but I have listed my preference in each ingredient list.

Saturated fats, such as vegetable shortening and lard, should be consumed in moderate amounts, as too much will begin to reduce the amount of "good" HDL-cholesterol in our systems. Vegetable shortening, because it is more highly refined than vegetable oil, fries with the least amount of odor, and I use it for most of my deep-frying. Lard is a very flavorful frying medium and is great when you want an old-fashioned taste. Vegetable oil is a more healthful alternative. If possible, use a professional-grade deep-frying oil. Previously available only through restaurant suppliers, it is now easy to find at wholesale grocers and price clubs in five-quart plastic containers. Of all the frying mediums I've tested, this left the least aroma and gave the best results. Five quarts may seem like a lot of deep-frying oil (you wouldn't want to use it like regular oil for other kinds of cooking), but if you are making a lot of special holiday dishes, it will be very handy. It also has a long shelf life.

Many cooks prefer peanut, canola, or soybean oils for deep-frying, none of which impart a strong taste to the food. When cooking Chinese food, I use peanut or soybean oil for their complementary flavors. Grapeseed oil, which many European chefs recommend, is a good deep-frying oil, but hard to find and expensive. To my taste, corn and safflower oils are a little too heavy for deep-frying. Never use Asian dark sesame or walnut oils—they are seasoning oils, not cooking oils, and will smoke at a low temperature.

Olive oil is an excellent choice, especially when cooking Italian specialties, but it will add its flavor to the food (which can be a good thing). Olive oil raises the "good" HDL-cholesterol level, so it's a healthy choice, too.

Unfortunately, deep-frying in olive oil is expensive—in America. In Italy, olive oil is cheap, and many of my Italian friends insist on using olive oil for deep-frying. They figure, sensibly, that if they only deep-fry for special occasions, why not use the best? When I deep-fry in olive oil, I am happy with a moderate-priced golden olive oil, and save the green-hued extra-virgin oil for the salad bowl.

Often, cooks make an issue out of an oil's smoking point. The smoking point is the temperature at which an oil starts to give off a light blue haze and "break down" into separate components that can cause it to acquire an off taste or even catch fire. However, deep-fried food should never be cooked above 400°F, which is near the smoking point of most oils. So as long as the oil doesn't get overheated, smoking isn't a real problem.

Some cooks strain, refrigerate, and reuse fat a few times before they finally throw it away, but I think that's a poor idea. I never use deep-frying fat a second time. Every time fat is heated, it breaks down a little more, which increases the fat's saturation level and affects its flavor, odor, smoking point, and flash point (the temperature at which it could ignite). Fat also picks up the flavor of whatever was cooked in it, so you could get shrimp-flavored cookies if you lose track. Just factor in the cost of fresh deep-frying fat along with the cost of the other ingredients, and do your tastebuds a favor.

Store oil and shortening in a dark, cool place, where it will keep for up to 3 months. Never store deep-frying fat of any kind (except lard) in the refrigerator. Oil solidifies when chilled, and would then need to be brought to room temperature to liquify. Chilled fat will splatter when heated, making a dangerous situation. If using lard, let it stand at room temperature for 1 hour before heating to remove the chill. I encourage you to buy fresh fat every time you deep-fry, and then you won't have to worry about where to store it for any length of time.

To discard vegetable oil, let it come to room temperature before pouring it into a large jar with a tight-fitting lid. To discard shortening, let it cool completely and return to its solid state. Then scrape it into its original container and dispose of it.

Setting Up

Mise en place is the French technique of preparing and assembling all the ingredients and utensils necessary to cook a dish before you start. It's a great procedure for any kind of cooking, but, boy, is it ever important with deep-frying. Nothing is worse than being ready to remove pieces of food from the deep fryer, only to find that you don't have a place to drain them.

First, make sure you have a way to transfer the food from the work area to the stove. A waxed paper–lined baking sheet is the easiest way for the food to make the trip from one spot to another.

You will also need a surface on which the fried food will be drained. A baking sheet lined with paper towels or brown paper bags is called for in some recipes. Other foods need to be elevated on a wire cake rack when draining, to keep steam from collecting under the coating and turning the crisp exterior soggy. This mimics the way restaurants drain deep-fried foods in wire baskets. Since the food doesn't touch any flat surfaces, it will stay crisper longer. To make a draining area, place a large wire cake rack over a jelly roll pan or sided baking sheet to hold the dripping oil. A large cake rack (mine is $16\frac{1}{2}$ by 13 inches) works best, or you can overlap two smaller cake racks.

A large wire-mesh skimmer is the best tool for retrieving deep-fried food. Slotted spoons tend to hold too much oil. Skimmers are available in a variety of sizes at Asian housewares stores and most Western kitchenware shops. (I bought my favorite one at a flea market in Tuscany, where they do a lot of deep-frying.)

Deep-frying baskets are fine when you are deep-frying a small amount of food. But don't be tempted to fill up the basket, as too much food will cause the fat temperature to drop too rapidly. Dip the basket in the fat first, *then* add the food, to keep the food from cooking right onto the basket.

Temperature control is one of the most important factors of deep-frying, as there are optimum temperatures for different foods. Always use the temperature suggested in each recipe. A deep-frying thermometer will make this task much simpler. Of all the different types of deep-frying thermometers (including glass tube–encased thermometers, and spring-operated dials with metal stems), my favorite is a mercury thermometer attached to a metal plaque (the plaque keeps the bottom of the thermometer stem from touching the bottom of the pot, which would give an inaccurate reading). No matter what type of thermometer you use, be sure it has a clip for attaching onto the pot. And never keep a thermometer in hot fat longer than necessary—if the fat overheats, the themometer could crack and the mercury will contaminate the fat.

If you are without a thermometer, the fat can be tested by adding a bread cube. If the bread cube browns in 1 minute, the temperature is about 350°F. Chinese cooks insert wooden chopsticks into the oil—if tiny bubbles surround the ends of the chopsticks, the oil is about 375°F. Also, when the fat is hot enough, the surface will shimmer slightly. But, a thermometer is always the most reliable choice.

As soon as the fat reaches the right temperature, add the food. It is important to carefully add the food to the hot fat so it doesn't splash. Never crowd food in the pot. The pieces should swim in the fat without touching. It is much better to cook the food in batches than all at once. If you're cooking on a stove, keep the heat on high to return the fat to its optimum cooking temperature, as it will have dropped from the addition of the food. And always allow the fat to return to the proper temperature before adding the next batch.

When you're ready to fry, preheat the oven to its lowest setting (anywhere from 150° to 200°F) to keep the first batch warm while frying the remaining food. After the first batch is drained, transfer the jelly roll pan, with the food on it, to the warm oven. Most fried food loses its appeal when it cools, and should be served as hot as possible. In fact, many cooks serve fried food one batch at a time, just as it comes out of the pot. This works well for people with an eat-in kitchen, but may be impractical for others.

Deep-frying on the stove does cause cooking odors, but the problem can be minimized (most electric fryers have odor filters). When I deep-fry in my loft, I run the air conditioner and the stove exhaust. When I cooked some of these recipes at my parents' home, whose California kitchen has large sliding doors leading outside, we just opened the doors wide to get good cross ventilation. My friend Harriet has the ultimate solution. She cooks in her electric deep-fryer outside on her backyard table.

small fry

snacks, nibbles & little bites

Saratoga Potato Chips with Caramelized Shallot Dip 18 • Mozzarella Cubes on Spaghetti Sticks with Pizzaola Sauce 21 • Root Vegetable Chips with Roasted Garlic Dip 22 • Little Meatballs with Salsa Verde 25 • Rice Crisps with Peanut-Lime Dipping Sauce 26 • Tostaditas with Ancho Salsa Roja 28 • Glittering Spiced Walnuts 30 • Coconut Shrimp with Pineapple-Mustard Dip 32 • Parmesan Pasta Nibbles 33 • Pork and Shrimp Balls with Sweet and Spicy Dipping Sauce 34

Saratoga Potato Chips
with Caramelized Shallot Dip

The ultimate deep-fried snack? I nominate potato chips with onion dip. Legend says that potato chips were invented by a Saratoga Springs, New York, chef in the mid-1850s, when he had to get a potato side dish on the table fast. Onion dip, stirred together from instant soup mix and sour cream, has been a party staple since the 1950s. But nothing beats homemade potato chips and a from-scratch version of the outré dip, made with deep-fried shallots. You'll need a mandoline to cut the potatoes to the proper paper-thin thickness.

1 To make the dip: Line a jelly roll pan with crumpled paper towels. In a deep Dutch oven, melt vegetable shortening over high heat to a depth of 2 to 3 inches and heat it to 350°F. If you have a frying basket to fit the Dutch oven, place the shallots in the basket. Deep-fry the shallots until golden brown, about 1 minute. Remove from the shortening (if you aren't using a basket, use a wire-mesh skimmer) and transfer to paper towels to drain until cool. (You may use the same shortening to fry the potato chips, but if there are small pieces of shallots floating in it, remove them. If necessary, carefully strain the shortening through a wire strainer into another pan, then return it to the Dutch oven.)

2 In a small bowl, combine the shallots, sour cream, chives, salt, and pepper. Cover and refrigerate for at least 1 hour to blend the flavors.

3 To make the chips: Using a mandoline, cut the potatoes into paper-thin rounds. As they are cut, place them in a bowl of cold water and let stand while heating the shortening.

4 Place a large wire cake rack over a jelly roll pan. Fill a roasting pan with crumpled paper towels for draining the fried chips. In a deep Dutch oven, melt vegetable shortening over high heat to a depth of 2 to 3 inches and heat it to 350°F.

continued ➥

Caramelized Sh...
Vegetable short...
   deep-frying
1 cup thinly sliced shallots
1 cup sour cream
3 tablespoons finely chopped fresh
   chives
1/4 teaspoon salt
1/4 teaspoon freshly ground pepper

Saratoga Potato Chips
1 pound baking (Idaho or russet)
   potatoes, peeled
Vegetable shortening or oil for deep-
   frying or leftover shortening from
   shallots, above
Salt for serving

5 Drain the potatoes well. Line a work surface with paper towels and spread with 1 layer of potatoes. Separate each new layer of potatoes with more paper towels and pat the potatoes completely dry.

6 In separate batches, without crowding, deep-fry the potatoes, stirring often with a wire-mesh strainer to separate the chips, until the chips are golden brown, 2 to 3 minutes. Using the skimmer, transfer the chips to the wire rack to drain briefly, then move them to the paper towels to remove excess oil. Separate each new layer of chips with more paper towels. The potato chips will crisp as they cool, and are best served at room temperature within 6 hours of frying. Just before serving, sprinkle with salt. Serve with the shallot dip.

MAKES 4 TO 6 APPETIZER SERVINGS

Don't salt deep-fried foods until just before serving, or the salt will make the food soggy.

Mozzarella Cubes

When I was catering, I passed countless hors d'oeuvres, many of them speared with toothpicks so they would be easy for the guests to pick up. I quickly tired of collecting the used toothpicks, and devised an edible toothpick in the form of a deep-fried spaghetti stick. What better way to illustrate this innovation than golden breaded mozzarella cubes served with an oregano-and-garlic-scented tomato sauce?

1 To make the sauce: In a small saucepan over medium heat, heat the oil. Add the onion and cook, stirring occasionally, until golden, about 4 minutes. Add the garlic and cook until fragrant, about 1 minute. Stir in the tomato sauce, water, oregano, basil, and red pepper flakes. Bring to a simmer and reduce heat to low. Simmer until slightly thickened, about 10 minutes. Set aside and keep warm. (The sauce can be prepared up to 1 day ahead, covered, and refrigerated. Reheat before serving.)

2 To make the cubes: Preheat the oven to 200°F. Line one baking sheet with waxed paper, and another baking sheet with paper towels. In a deep Dutch oven, melt vegetable shortening over high heat to a depth of 2 to 3 inches and heat it to 365°F.

3 Place the flour in a shallow bowl. Beat the eggs in another shallow bowl. Place the bread crumbs in a third shallow bowl. One at a time, roll each mozzarella cube in the flour, dip in the eggs, then coat completely with the bread crumbs. Set aside on the waxed paper.

4 Deep-fry the spaghetti until golden brown, about 2 minutes. Using a wire-mesh skimmer, transfer to the paper towels to drain and cool. In batches, without crowding, deep-fry the mozzarella cubes until golden brown, about 3 minutes. Using the skimmer, transfer to the paper towels and keep warm in the oven while frying the rest.

5 To serve, spear each cube with a spaghetti stick. Serve immediately, with a bowl of the warm sauce for dipping.

MAKES 36 CUBES (4 TO 6 APPETIZER SERVINGS)

Pizzaola Sauce

1 tablespoon olive oil
1/3 cup finely chopped onion
1 garlic clove, crushed through a press
1 cup tomato sauce
1/4 cup water
1 teaspoon dried oregano
1/2 teaspoon dried basil
1/4 teaspoon hot red pepper flakes

Mozzarella Cubes

1 pound mozzarella cheese, preferably fresh, cut into thirty-six 1/2-inch cubes
1/2 cup all-purpose flour
3 large eggs, beaten
3/4 cup dried Italian-seasoned bread crumbs

About 10 strands spaghetti, broken into thirty-six 3-inch lengths
Vegetable shortening or oil for deep-frying

Root Vegetable Chips

Carrots, parsnips, beets, taro, and lotus root all make chips that are not only delicious, but colorful, to boot. Make an assortment, and you'll have a rainbow in a bowl. The ricotta-garlic dip is the perfect partner, and one of the most-requested standards from my extensive dip-spread repertoire.

1 To make the dip: Preheat the oven to 400°F. Cut the garlic in half horizontally, keeping the head as intact as possible—do not peel the garlic. Drizzle the cut surfaces with the oil and season with a sprinkle of salt and pepper. Put the two halves back together to re-form the garlic head. Wrap tightly in aluminum foil. Bake until the garlic is tender and the cloves have turned golden beige, 35 to 45 minutes. Unwrap the garlic and let cool completely. Squeeze the garlic pulp out of the skins into a small bowl, discarding the skins.

2 Using a fork, mash the garlic pulp until smooth. Stir in the ricotta, Parmigiano, and sour cream. Season with salt and pepper to taste. Let stand for 30 minutes at room temperature to blend the flavors. (The dip can be prepared 1 day ahead, covered, and refrigerated. Let it come to room temperature before serving.)

3 To make the chips: Using a mandoline or plastic V-slicer, cut the root vegetables as directed below. The slices should be almost paper-thin, less than $1/16$ inch. As the vegetables are sliced, place each kind in a separate large bowl of cold water and let stand for 30 minutes to remove excess starch.

Carrots and parsnips: Peel and cut lengthwise into very thin strips.
Beets: Rub your hands lightly with vegetable oil to keep the beet juices from staining your skin. Peel the beets and cut crosswise into very thin rounds.
Lotus roots: These can be found at Asian grocers, and make very interesting chips with random holes throughout. Peel and cut crosswise into very thin rounds.

continued ➨

Roasted Garlic Dip

1 large head garlic, with firm, plump cloves
1 teaspoon extra-virgin olive oil
Salt and freshly ground pepper to taste
1 cup ricotta cheese
$1/2$ cup freshly grated Parmigiano-Reggiano cheese
$1/2$ cup sour cream

Root Vegetable Chips

$1\frac{1}{2}$ pounds assorted root vegetables, such as carrots, parsnips, beets, lotus roots, and taro
Vegetable shortening or oil for deep-frying

Taro: Also known as yautia, this root vegetable can be purchased at Latino and Asian markets. Fried taro chips have a slight purple tinge. Peel and cut crosswise into very thin rounds.

4 Drain the vegetables well. Spread them out between layers of paper towels and pat *completely dry.*

5 Place a large wire cake rack over a jelly roll pan. Fill a large roasting pan with a double thickness of crumpled paper towels. In a deep Dutch oven, melt vegetable shortening over high heat to a depth of 2 to 3 inches and heat it to 350°F.

6 In separate batches, without crowding, deep-fry the vegetables, stirring often with a wire-mesh skimmer to separate the chips, until the chips are golden brown, 2 to 3 minutes. (If you are frying beets, fry them last, as their color may leach into the oil.) Using the skimmer, transfer the chips to the wire racks to drain briefly, then move them to the roasting pan with paper towels to remove excess oil. Separate each new layer of chips with more paper towels. The chips will crisp as they cool, and are best served at room temperature within 6 hours of frying. Just before serving, sprinkle with salt and pepper, and serve with the ricotta dip.

MAKES 6 TO 8 APPETIZER SERVINGS

Little Meatballs

These aren't the average meatballs served with a tomato sauce, but were created as an antipasto to be dipped in salsa verde, a piquant Italian parsley sauce. Both the meatballs and sauce can be prepared ahead of serving, but don't coat the meatballs until ready to fry them.

1 To make the salsa: In a blender, combine all of the ingredients except the oil. With the machine running, gradually add the oil through the cover opening until the sauce is smooth and thick. Transfer to a small bowl, cover, and let stand for at least 30 minutes for the flavors to blend. (The salsa can be prepared up to 1 day ahead, covered, and refrigerated. Serve at room temperature.)

2 To make the meatballs: Line a baking sheet with waxed paper. In a medium bowl, beat together $\frac{1}{2}$ cup of the bread crumbs, 1 egg, and the milk. Let stand for 5 minutes. Add the ground round, sausage, cheese, onion, parsley, garlic, salt, and pepper and mix with your hands until well combined. Using a heaping teaspoonful for each, form into balls and place on waxed paper. You should have about 36 bite-sized meatballs.

3 Place the remaining $1\frac{1}{2}$ cups bread crumbs in a deep plate. In another deep plate, whisk the remaining 2 eggs until well beaten. One at a time, dip the meatballs in the eggs, then coat with the bread crumbs, patting to make the crumbs adhere. Return to the waxed paper.

4 Line another baking sheet with paper towels. In a deep Dutch oven, melt vegetable shortening to a depth of 2 to 3 inches and heat it to 365°F. In batches, without crowding, deep-fry the meatballs until golden brown, about 3 minutes. Using a wire-mesh skimmer, transfer to the paper towels. Serve warm or at room temperature, with the salsa verde.

MAKES 6 TO 8 APPETIZER SERVINGS

Salsa Verde

$\frac{1}{2}$ cup packed chopped fresh parsley
$\frac{1}{4}$ cup sliced blanched almonds
$1\frac{1}{2}$ teaspoons Dijon mustard
$1\frac{1}{2}$ teaspoons fresh lemon juice
1 teaspoon anchovy paste
1 garlic clove, peeled
$\frac{1}{4}$ teaspoon salt
$\frac{1}{8}$ teaspoon freshly ground pepper
$\frac{1}{2}$ cup extra-virgin olive oil

Little Meatballs

2 cups fresh bread crumbs (prepared in a blender or food processor from slightly stale bread)
3 large eggs
2 tablespoons milk
8 ounces ground round (15 percent lean)
8 ounces Italian pork sausage, casings removed
$\frac{1}{4}$ cup freshly grated Parmigiano-Reggiano cheese
$\frac{1}{4}$ cup finely chopped onion
2 tablespoons finely chopped fresh parsley
1 garlic clove, crushed through a press
$\frac{1}{2}$ teaspoon salt
$\frac{1}{4}$ teaspoon freshly ground pepper
Vegetable shortening or oil for deep-frying

Rice Crisps
with Peanut-Lime Dipping Sauce

Rice Crisps
1 cup long-grain white rice
1/4 teaspoon salt
2 cups water

Peanut-Lime Dipping Sauce
1/3 cup peanut butter
1/4 cup hoisin sauce
1/4 cup homemade or canned
    low-salt chicken broth
1 tablespoon Japanese soy sauce
2 tablespoons fresh lime juice
Grated zest of 1 lime
1/2 teaspoon Asian chili paste
    with garlic

Vegetable shortening or oil for
    deep-frying

Asian cooks *want* a thick crust of rice to form on the bottom of the cooking pot, because they know it can be fried into a crunchy snack. While many Asian grocers carry rice crusts (about 3 inches square, not to be confused with rice cakes) for frying, a recipe comes in handy. If you make your own, you'll need to start a day before you want to eat the crisps. Served with a Thai-inspired peanut sauce and a cold beer, these are easy to eat by the bucketful.

1 To make the rice crisps the day before serving: In a medium, heavy saucepan (preferably nonstick and 9 inches in diameter), bring the rice, salt and water to a boil over high heat. Reduce heat to low, cover, and cook until the rice is tender and absorbs all the liquid, about 20 minutes. Uncover and cook until the rice dries into crust that pulls away from the sides of the saucepan, about 1 hour. Let the rice crust cool in the pan.

2 Using a blunt knife, pry the crust out of the saucepan, trying to keep it intact. Place on a wire cake rack and let stand in a turned-off gas oven until completely dry, at least 8 hours and preferably overnight. Or, heat an electric oven at its lowest setting for 10 minutes, then turn it off before placing the rice inside. (If the weather is humid or damp, dry the rice out more quickly by occasionally turning the oven on its lowest setting for 5 minutes, then turning it off.) The rice should be dried out, but not toasted. Cut the rice crust into 1 1/2-inch squares, discarding any crumbs, and set aside.

3 To make the dipping sauce: Whisk all the ingredients together in a small bowl. Let stand at room temperature for 30 minutes to blend the flavors. (The sauce will thicken on standing. If necessary, thin with additional broth or water.)

4 In a deep Dutch oven, melt vegetable shortening over high heat to a depth of 2 to 3 inches and heat it to 365°F. Line a baking sheet with paper towels. In batches, without crowding, deep-fry the rice crust squares until puffed and golden, about 3 minutes. Using a wire-mesh skimmer, transfer to the paper towels to drain. Let cool completely. (The crisps can be prepared up to 6 hours ahead, stored uncovered at room temperature.) Serve the crisps with the dipping sauce.

MAKES 4 TO 6 APPETIZER SERVINGS

Tostaditas
with Ancho Salsa Roja

Ancho Salsa Roja

10 dried New Mexico chilies
(about 2½ ounces)
1 small onion, chopped
2 garlic cloves, crushed through
a press
1 teaspoon dried oregano
¼ teaspoon ground cumin
1 tablespoon olive oil
2 tablespoons finely chopped
fresh cilantro
¼ teaspoon salt

Tostaditas

12 corn tortillas, cut into sixths
Vegetable shortening or oil for
deep-frying

It is no news that tortilla chips and salsa are irresistible. Chunky tomato salsas are popular, but I like to dip my chips in this thin sauce, which is served in New Mexican restaurants. It is brick-red and intense with the flavor of local dried chilies. Choose a heat level that you can tolerate—they should be labeled mild, medium, or hot. As for the tortillas, they are best if allowed to stale slightly before frying. Rather than air-drying them, I bake them briefly. There are a lot of mediocre, preservative-laden tortillas on the market, so when you find a brand you like, save the label so you'll remember it the next time you are tortilla shopping.

1 To make the salsa: Heat a large, empty skillet over medium-high heat. Break the chilies open and discard the seeds and stems. Open up the chilies and place them in the skillet. In batches, toast the chilies, occasionally turning and pressing them flat with a metal spatula, until they are pliable and the color has deepened, about 1 minute. They should be toasted, but not scorched. Place the toasted chilies in a medium bowl and cover with boiling water. Let stand until the chilies soften, about 20 minutes. Drain, reserving the soaking liquid.

2 In a blender, combine the drained chiles, onion, garlic, oregano, and cumin. With the machine running, add enough of the soaking liquid to make a smooth puree, about ¾ cup.

3 In a medium nonstick skillet over medium heat, heat the olive oil. Add the chili puree and cook, stirring almost constantly, until thickened, about 3 minutes. Transfer to a small bowl and stir in the cilantro and salt. (The sauce can be prepared up to 2 days ahead, cooled, covered, and refrigerated. Serve at room temperature.)

4 To make the tostaditas: Position racks in the center and top third of the oven and preheat the oven to 350°F. Spread the tortilla wedges on 2 baking sheets. Bake, switching the positions of the sheets from top to bottom halfway through baking, until the tortillas are slightly dried, about 10 minutes. Remove from the oven and let cool.

5 Line 2 baking sheets with paper towels and set aside. In a deep Dutch oven, melt vegetable shortening over high heat to a depth of 2 to 3 inches and heat it to 365°F. In batches, without crowding, deep-fry the tortillas until golden brown, less than 1 minute. Using a wire-mesh skimmer, transfer to the paper towels to dry. (The chips can be prepared up to 8 hours ahead, stored uncovered at room temperature.) Just before serving, sprinkle the chips with salt. Serve with the sauce for dipping.

MAKES 4 TO 6 APPETIZER SERVINGS

VARIATION: STIR 1/2 CUP PLAIN YOGURT INTO THE COOLED SALSA. THIS MAKES A MELLOWER DIP THAT SOME COOKS MAY PREFER.

Glittering Spiced Walnuts

Spice Mixture

1 whole star anise pod (use 6 or 7 "points" if pod is broken)

1/2 teaspoon ground cinnamon

1/2 teaspoon coriander seed

1/2 teaspoon whole Szechuan peppercorns

1/4 teaspoon fennel seeds

4 whole cloves

1/8 teaspoon cayenne pepper

Vegetable shortening or oil for deep-frying

1 pound walnut halves, preferably extra-fancy

1/2 cup sugar

Fine sea salt or iodized salt for sprinkling

For gift-giving, use the very best extra-fancy walnut halves. They are available at nut shops and bakery suppliers, or by mail order from A. L. Bazzini Co., 339 Greenwich Street, New York, NY 10013, (212) 334-1280.

To remove the flavor of coffee from a coffee grinder before grinding spices—or conversely, to absorb spice flavor to use the grinder again for coffee—place 1/4 cup granulated sugar in the grinder, process it until powdery, and discard.

One of my most popular dishes: Walnuts with a sheer sugar coating and seasoned with aromatic spices. One of my cooking students reports that he now makes at least 50 pounds every Christmas to sell to friends, raising funds for his favorite charity. If making this recipe in quantity, be sure to have plenty of vegetable shortening handy, as the sugar in the nuts will "caramelize" the oil, necessitating fresh shortening after each 2 or 3 pounds. For the best results, use walnut halves—small walnut pieces will burn.

1 To make the spice mixture: Finely grind all the spices in a spice grinder or electric coffee grinder. Set aside.

2 Place an empty baking sheet next to the stove. Line a second baking sheet with paper towels. In a deep Dutch oven, melt shortening over high heat to a depth of 2 to 3 inches and heat it to 365°F.

3 Meanwhile, bring a medium saucepan of water to a boil over high heat. Add the walnuts and cook for 1 minute only. The water does not have to return to a boil. (This removes excess bitterness.) Drain in a large colander. Do not rinse. Immediately toss the walnuts with the sugar in the colander until the hot water clinging to the walnuts melts the sugar to form a thin glaze.

4 In two batches, deep-fry the walnuts until golden, about 3 minutes. Using a wire-mesh skimmer, transfer the walnuts to the unlined baking sheet (the hot walnuts would stick to paper towels) and let cool completely. When cooled, transfer the walnuts to the paper towels and pat with more towels to drain excess oil.

5 Put the walnuts in a bowl. While tossing the nuts, sift the spice mixture through a fine-meshed sieve over them. Discard the hulls left in the sieve. Season the walnuts with the salt. (The walnuts can be prepared up to 1 week ahead, stored in an airtight container at room temperature.)

Makes 1 pound (6 to 8 appetizer servings)

Coconut Shrimp
with Pineapple-Mustard Dip

Pineapple-Mustard Dip
½ cup pineapple preserves
3 tablespoons Dijon mustard

Coconut Batter
1 cup all-purpose flour
1 teaspoon baking powder
1½ teaspoons Madras-style curry
    powder
½ teaspoon salt
⅛ teaspoon cayenne pepper
1¼ cups flat lager beer
2 large eggs, beaten
1 cup unsweetened desiccated
    coconut (available at natural
    foods stores)

1 pound extra-large to large shrimp,
    peeled (leave tail segment
    attached) and deveined
Vegetable shortening or oil for
    deep-frying

This recipe for one of the classic deep-fried appetizers also appears in my book *Simply Shrimp*. It bears repeating—prepared with a light beer batter and unsweetened coconut, I think it's the best version around. The shrimp are also great dunked in Peanut-Lime Dipping Sauce (page 26), so you might want to serve both sauces and offer guests a choice.

1 To make the dip: In a small saucepan, bring the preserves to a simmer over medium heat, stirring constantly. Remove from heat and stir in the mustard. Keep the dip warm. (The dip can be prepared up to 4 hours ahead, and reheated gently before serving.)

2 To make the batter: In a medium bowl, whisk the flour, baking powder, curry powder, salt, and cayenne together. Add the beer and eggs and stir with a spoon just until combined (do not overmix). Fold in ½ cup of the coconut. Put the remaining coconut in a deep plate.

3 Preheat the oven to 200°F. Place a large wire cake rack over a jelly roll pan. In a deep Dutch oven, melt vegetable shortening over high heat to a depth of 2 to 3 inches and heat it to 360°F.

4 In 2 or 3 batches, dip each shrimp in the batter, letting the excess batter drip back into the bowl, then roll the shrimp in the coconut. Deep-fry without crowding, until golden, 2 to 3 minutes. Using a wire-mesh skimmer, transfer the shrimp to the wire rack and keep warm in the oven until all the shrimp are deep-fried. Serve immediately, with the warm pineapple-mustard dip.

MAKES 6 TO 8 APPETIZER SERVINGS

Parmesan Pasta Nibbles

This is another snack that is hard to stop eating once you get started: One crunchy bite leads to another. You can experiment with different kinds of pasta, but flavored ones have the most punch, as does real Italian Parmesan.

1 In a large pot of salted boiling water, cook the pasta, stirring occasionally, until tender, about 9 minutes. Drain, shaking the colander well to remove excess water. Spread the pasta out on a clean kitchen towel and pat dry.

2 Line a jelly roll pan with paper towels. In a deep Dutch oven, melt vegetable shortening over high heat to a depth of 2 to 3 inches and heat it to 350°F. In 2 batches, deep-fry the pasta until crisp, 2 to 3 minutes. Using a wire-mesh skimmer, transfer to the paper towels to drain. In a large bowl, drizzle the pasta with the olive oil.

3 In a large paper bag, combine the cheese, basil, oregano, garlic powder, salt, and cayenne. Add the pasta, close the bag, and shake to coat the pasta with the cheese mixture. Transfer to a serving bowl. (The pasta nibbles can be prepared up to 1 day ahead and kept stored at room temperature in an airtight container.)

MAKES 8 SNACK SERVINGS

8 ounces tomato-and-basil or tricolored (spinach, tomato, and plain) short corkscrew-shaped pasta (often called rotini or fusilli)
Vegetable shortening or oil for deep-frying
2 tablespoons extra-virgin olive oil
½ cup freshly grated Parmigiano-Reggiano cheese
2 teaspoons dried basil
2 teaspoons dried oregano
½ teaspoon garlic powder
½ teaspoon salt
¼ teaspoon cayenne pepper

with Sweet and Spicy Dipping Sauce
Pork and Shrimp Balls

Sweet and Spicy Dipping Sauce

½ cup water

¼ cup rice vinegar

3 tablespoons Asian fish sauce
(nam pla or nuoc mam)

3 tablespoons packed light
brown sugar

2 quarter-sized pieces fresh ginger,
cut into thin sticks

1 garlic clove, pressed

1 teaspoon cornstarch dissolved in
2 tablespoons water

1 or 2 Thai bird or serrano chilies, or 1
jalapeño chili, cut into thin rounds

Pork and Shrimp Balls

8 ounces medium shrimp, peeled
and deveined

8 ounces ground pork

2 tablespoons finely chopped cilantro
sprigs with stems

1 tablespoon Asian fish sauce (nam
pla or nuoc mam)

2 teaspoons shredded fresh ginger
(use the coarse holes of a box
grater)

1 teaspoon minced seeded Thai or
serrano chili

1 garlic clove, pressed

½ cup cornstarch

Vegetable shortening or oil for
deep-frying

2 heads Boston lettuce, separated
into whole leaves

Pork and shrimp are sweet, lush ingredients that can stand up to strong Asian seasonings like ginger, cilantro, and chilies. These morsels are an enticing first course for a Pacific Rim dinner, or pass them on a platter as a cocktail-time nibble.

1 To make the sauce: In a small saucepan, bring the water, vinegar, fish sauce, brown sugar, ginger, and garlic to a simmer over medium heat. Stir in the cornstarch mixture and stir until boiling and lightly thickened. Transfer to a small bowl and stir in the chili rounds. Let stand for 30 minutes for the flavors to blend. (The sauce can be prepared up to 8 hours ahead of serving and kept at room temperature.)

2 To make the pork and shrimp balls: Line a baking sheet with waxed paper. In a food processor, pulse the shrimp until it forms a paste. Add the pork, cilantro, fish sauce, ginger, chili, and garlic. Pulse until combined. Using a heaping tablespoonful for each, form the paste into 1-inch balls and place on the waxed paper. (The balls can be covered and refrigerated for up to 8 hours.)

3 Preheat the oven to 200°F. Line a jelly roll pan with paper towels. In a deep Dutch oven, melt shortening over high heat to a depth of 2 inches and heat it to 365°F.

4 Place the cornstarch in a deep plate and roll the balls in the cornstarch to coat them evenly. In batches, without crowding, deep-fry the balls until golden brown, 3 to 4 minutes. Using a wire-mesh skimmer, transfer the balls to the paper towels to drain. Keep warm in the oven while frying the remaining balls. Serve the hot pork and shrimp balls with the lettuce leaves, so guests can wrap the balls in the leaves and dip the packet into the sauce.

MAKES ABOUT 24 BALLS

upper crust

savory pies, turnovers, rolls & dumplings

Calzonetti with Sun-Dried Tomato and Mozzarella Filling 38 • Toasted Ravioli with Tomato Sauce 40 • Chicken and Olive Empanadas 42 • Cauliflower Samosas with Cilantro Chutney 44 • Vegetarian Moo Shu Egg Rolls 46 • Goat Cheese Wontons with Tomato-Herb Salsa 49 • Fried Dough Knots with Garlic Oil 50 • Crab Spring Rolls with Sweet Garlic Sauce 52 • Beef and Cabbage Piroshki 55

Calzonetti

Calzonetti Dough

1½ teaspoons active dry yeast
¼ cup warm (105° to 115°F) water
3 cups unbleached flour
¾ teaspoon salt
2 tablespoons extra-virgin olive oil
⅔ cup cold water

Mozzarella Filling

1 cup (4 ounces) shredded
    mozzarella cheese
⅔ cup chopped black Mediterranean
    olives
½ cup (3 ounces) chopped sun-dried
    tomatoes (not oil-packed)
2 tablespoons chopped fresh basil
1 garlic clove, crushed through a
    press
¼ teaspoon hot red pepper flakes

1 large egg yolk beaten with
    1 teaspoon water
Olive oil or vegetable oil for
    deep-frying

Calzones are most familiar to American eaters as big baked half-moons of stuffed pizza. In southern Italy, they are also formed into calzonetti, little pies small enough to disappear in a couple of bites. Add these to your antipasto selection the next time you entertain Italian style.

1 To make the dough: In a small bowl, sprinkle the yeast over the warm water and let stand until creamy, about 5 minutes. Stir to dissolve the yeast.

2 In a food processor, pulse the flour and salt to combine. With the machine running, add the yeast mixture and oil, and enough water to form a ball of dough on top of the blade (there may be smaller particles of dough in the bowl as well as the large ball). If the dough is too wet or too dry, it will not form a ball. Feel the dough, and if it is sticky and wet, add additional flour, 2 tablespoons at a time, processing after each addition, until the dough forms a ball. If it seems too dry, follow the same procedure, adding additional water 1 tablespoon at a time. Process the ball of dough for 45 seconds. To make the dough by hand, place the flour and salt in a large bowl. Stir in the yeast mixture and oil, and enough water to form a shaggy dough. Turn the dough out onto a lightly floured surface and knead until smooth and elastic, about 10 minutes.

3 Lightly grease a medium bowl with shortening. Form the dough into a ball and place in the bowl, turning the dough to coat it with the shortening. Cover the bowl with plastic wrap and let rise in a warm place until almost doubled, or until a finger inserted ½ inch into the dough leaves an impression, about 1½ hours.

4 Meanwhile, to make the filling: In a medium bowl, mix the cheese, olives, sun-dried tomatoes, basil, garlic, and red pepper flakes together.

5 Punch down the dough. On a lightly floured surface, knead the dough a few times. Cut the dough into 20 pieces and roll each portion into a walnut-sized ball. Cover the balls of dough with plastic wrap.

6 Line 2 baking sheets with clean kitchen towels and dust the towels with flour. Working with 1 ball of dough at a time, keeping the remaining dough covered, roll the dough out on a very lightly floured surface (the oil in the dough keeps it from sticking) into a 5-inch round. Place 1 tablespoon of the filling on the bottom half of the round, about $\frac{1}{2}$ inch from the edge. Brush the edges of the dough with the egg yolk mixture. Fold the dough over to enclose the filling. Press the edges of the dough with the tines of a fork to seal. Transfer to a floured kitchen towel and cover loosely with plastic wrap. Repeat the procedure with the remaining dough and filling.

7 Line another baking sheet with paper towels. In a deep Dutch oven, heat 2 to 3 inches of oil over high heat to 365°F. In batches, without crowding, deep-fry the calzonetti until golden brown, about 3 minutes. Using a wire-mesh skimmer, transfer to the paper towels to drain. Serve warm or at room temperature.

MAKES 20 CALZONETTI

Fried ravioli can be found in almost every St. Louis restaurant, but especially on the Hill, the Italian neighborhood. It seems to have originated in Sicily, where fried ravioli, filled with a sweet filling, are a Christmas sweet (see page 128).

1 To make the tomato sauce: In a medium saucepan over medium heat, heat the oil and cook the onion and garlic, stirring often, until softened, about 5 minutes. Add the tomato puree, stock, wine, tomato paste, basil, oregano, and red pepper flakes. Bring to a simmer and reduce heat to low. Simmer, uncovered, until slightly thickened, about 45 minutes.

2 Preheat the oven to 200°F. Line a baking sheet with waxed paper. Place a large wire cake rack over a jelly roll pan. In a deep Dutch oven, melt vegetable shortening over high heat to a depth of 2 to 3 inches and heat to 375°F.

3 To toast the ravioli: In a shallow bowl, beat the milk and eggs together. Put the bread crumbs in another shallow bowl. One at a time, coat the ravioli with the egg mixture, then with the bread crumbs, and place on the waxed paper.

4 In batches, without crowding, deep-fry the ravioli until golden brown, about 3 minutes. Using a wire-mesh skimmer, transfer the ravioli to the wire rack and keep warm in the oven while frying the rest. Serve warm, not piping hot (the cheese could burn you), with the tomato sauce for dipping.

MAKES 6 TO 8 APPETIZER SERVINGS

Tomato Sauce
1 tablespoon olive oil
1 medium onion, chopped
1 garlic clove, crushed through a press
1 cup tomato puree
3/4 cup beef stock
1/2 cup hearty red wine, such as Zinfandel
1/4 cup tomato paste
1 teaspoon dried basil
1 teaspoon dried oregano
1/4 teaspoon hot red pepper flakes

Toasted Ravioli
Vegetable shortening or oil for deep-frying
1/2 cup milk
2 large eggs, beaten
3/4 cup dried bread crumbs
24 cheese-filled ravioli (about 8 ounces)

Chicken and Olive Empanadas

Empanada Dough
3 cups all-purpose flour
3/4 teaspoon salt
3/4 cup (1 1/2 sticks) cold unsalted butter, cut into 1/2-inch pieces
1/2 cup ice water
1 large egg yolk

Chicken and Olive Filling
2 tablespoons olive oil
1 medium onion, finely chopped
1 garlic clove, pressed
1 pound ground chicken or turkey (not ground turkey breast)
2 tablespoons tomato paste
1/3 cup dry sherry
1 teaspoon dried oregano
1/2 teaspoon sweet Hungarian paprika
3/4 teaspoon salt
1/2 teaspoon freshly ground pepper
1/2 cup thinly sliced pimiento-stuffed green olives
3 tablespoons nonpareil capers, rinsed (if using larger capers, chop them)
3 tablespoons currants or chopped raisins

1 large egg yolk beaten with 1 teaspoon water
Vegetable shortening or oil for deep-frying

When you need a big batch of hors d'oeuvres for a bash, these empanadas, with their sweet-savory filling and light, flaky crust, are hard to beat. They can be made ahead and frozen, and reheated for serving. If you need a smaller amount, reduce the filling by half, but make the entire amount of dough and freeze the remainder for up to 3 months for another use (it makes great pie dough).

1 To make the dough: In a large bowl, combine the flour and salt. Add the butter. Using a pastry cutter, cut in the butter until the mixture resembles coarse meal with a few pea-sized pieces. In a glass measuring cup, whisk the ice water and egg yolk together. Tossing the flour mixture with a fork, gradually add the liquid just until the dough is completely moistened and holds together without crumbling when pressed between your fingers. Form the dough into a thick disk. Wrap in waxed paper and refrigerate for 30 minutes. (The dough can be prepared up to 1 day ahead. If the dough is very cold and hard, let stand at room temperature for 10 minutes before rolling out.)

2 To make the filling: In a large skillet over medium-high heat, heat the oil. Add the onion and garlic and cook until softened, about 3 minutes. Add the chicken or turkey and cook, stirring often and breaking up the meat with the side of a spoon, until it loses its pink color and is cooked through, about 6 minutes. In a small bowl, dissolve the tomato paste in the sherry. Stir into the skillet with the oregano, paprika, salt, and pepper. Cook until the mixture looks somewhat dry, about 1 minute. Transfer to a medium bowl and stir in the olives, capers, and currants or raisins. Let cool completely.

3 Line 2 large baking sheets with waxed paper. Divide the dough into thirds. Keeping the remaining dough refrigerated, roll 1 piece at a time out on a lightly floured surface until 1/16 inch thick. Using a 3-inch round biscuit cutter, cut out rounds of the dough. Place 1 scant teaspoon of the cooled filling on the bottom half of each round. Brush the edges lightly with the yolk mixture, fold over to enclose the filling, and seal the edges by pressing with the tines of a fork. Place the empanadas on the prepared baking sheets and cover loosely with plastic wrap. Repeat with the remaining dough (gathering up the dough scraps and re-rolling as needed) and filling. Refrigerate the empanadas until ready to fry. (The empanadas can be prepared to this point up to 2 weeks ahead, covered tightly with plastic wrap and overwrapped with aluminum foil, and frozen. Thaw in the refrigerator overnight before deep-frying.)

4 Preheat the oven to 170°F. Line 2 baking sheets with paper towels. In a deep Dutch oven, melt vegetable shortening over high heat to a depth of 2 to 3 inches and heat it to 365°F. In batches, without crowding, deep-fry the empanadas until golden brown, about 3 minutes. Using a wire-mesh skimmer, transfer to the paper towels to drain and keep warm in the oven for up to 1 hour. (Or, let the empanadas cool. Cover and refrigerate for up to 8 hours. To reheat, bake in a preheated 350°F oven until heated through, about 10 minutes.) Serve the empanadas warm.

NOTE: THE FRIED EMPANADAS CAN BE MADE UP TO 2 WEEKS AHEAD AND FROZEN. PLACE IN A SINGLE LAYER ON WAXED PAPER—LINED BAKING SHEETS. COVER TIGHTLY WITH PLASTIC WRAP AND OVERWRAP WITH ALUMINUM FOIL. THAW OVERNIGHT IN THE REFRIGERATOR. TO REHEAT, BAKE IN A PREHEATED 350°F OVEN UNTIL HEATED THROUGH, ABOUT 10 MINUTES.

MAKES ABOUT 100 EMPANADAS

Cauliflower Samosas
with Cilantro Chutney

Cauliflower Filling
1 small head cauliflower (1½ pounds),
   broken into florets
2 tablespoons vegetable oil
1 large onion, chopped
2 teaspoons minced fresh ginger
2 garlic cloves, minced
¾ teaspoon salt
½ teaspoon ground coriander
½ teaspoon ground cumin
½ teaspoon Madras-style
   curry powder
¾ teaspoon fennel seed, crushed in
   a mortar or under a heavy skillet
¼ teaspoon ground turmeric
¼ teaspoon cayenne pepper

Cilantro Chutney
¾ cup chopped fresh cilantro
¼ cup fresh lemon juice
1 serrano or jalapeño chili,
   seeded and minced
¼ teaspoon salt

Samosa Dough
1½ cups all-purpose flour
1½ cups whole-wheat flour
1¼ teaspoons salt
3 tablespoons vegetable oil, plus
   additional for brushing
1 cup plus 2 tablespoons water

Vegetable shortening or oil for
   deep-frying

These distinctive cone-shaped Indian turnovers are often stuffed with potatoes and peas, but I devised this lighter cauliflower version. Whole-wheat flour is included in the samosa dough to make a firmer crust that doesn't get soggy in contact with the moist filling.

1 To make the filling: In a large saucepan of lightly salted boiling water, cook the cauliflower until tender, about 10 minutes. Drain and rinse under cold water. Finely chop the cauliflower with a large knife (don't use a food processor, which could puree the cauliflower). Place in a fine sieve and press gently to remove excess water. Set aside.

2 In a large skillet over medium heat, heat the oil. Add the onion and cook until golden brown, about 6 minutes. Reduce heat to medium-low and stir in the ginger, garlic, salt, coriander, cumin, curry powder, fennel, turmeric, and cayenne. Add the reserved cauliflower and stir constantly until well coated with the spices, about 1 minute. The cauliflower mixture should be fine-textured and dry, but not mashed. Let cool completely.

3 Meanwhile, make the chutney: In a small bowl, combine the cilantro, lemon juice, jalapeño, and salt. Cover and let stand at room temperature for up to 4 hours until ready to serve.

4 To make the dough: In a food processor, pulse the flour, whole-wheat flour, and salt to combine. In a glass measuring cup, mix the 3 tablespoons oil with the water. With the machine running, pour the liquid through the feed tube and process until the dough forms a large ball on top of the blade (there may be a few stray bits of dough in addition to the dough in the work bowl). If the dough is too dry or wet, the dough will not form a ball. If the dough feels wet and sticky, add additional flour, 1 tablespoon at a time, and process after each addition. If the dough feels dry and crumbly, follow the same procedure, adding additional water, 1 tablespoon at a time. To make the dough by hand, put the flours and salt in a large bowl. Stir in the oil and enough water to form a stiff dough. Turn out onto a lightly floured surface and knead until smooth and firm, about 10 minutes.

5 On an unfloured work surface, knead the dough briefly until smooth. Form into a ball, place on the work surface, and brush the top lightly with oil. Cover loosely with plastic wrap. Let stand for 5 minutes.

6 To make the samosas, dust 2 baking sheets with flour. Pinch off enough dough to roll into a 1¼-inch ball. Keeping the remaining dough covered, flatten the dough and roll it into a 5-inch round. With a sharp knife, cut the round in half crosswise to make 2 semicircles.

7 Moisten the straight edge of 1 semicircle with cold water. Lift up the ends of the straight edge to meet and overlap slightly, forming a cone shape. Press the overlapping seam of dough to seal. Place about 1 teaspoon filling into the cone. Pinch the open top of the cone shut, then press with the tines of a fork to seal. Place the samosa on a baking sheet. Repeat with the other semicircle, then the remaining dough and filling.

8 Preheat the oven to 200°F. Line 2 baking sheets with paper towels. In a deep Dutch oven, melt vegetable shortening over high heat to a depth of 2 to 3 inches and heat it to 365°F. In batches, without crowding, deep-fry the samosas until golden brown, about 3 minutes. Using a wire-mesh skimmer, transfer the samosas to the paper towels to drain. Serve warm, with the chutney for dipping.

MAKES 60 SAMOSAS

Vegetarian Moo Shu Egg Rolls

When recently faced with using up a container of leftover moo shu vegetables, I wrapped the veggies in egg roll skins and deep-fried them for an almost-instant appetizer. Served with little bowls of bottled Asian condiments, the result was so successful that now I stir-fry the vegetables from scratch. I leave out some moo sho ingredients like tree ear fungus and lily buds, but if you like, you can add them to the filling.

1 In a small bowl, cover the dried mushrooms with very hot water. Let stand until softened, about 30 minutes. Drain, remove and discard the stems, and cut the mushrooms into 1/4-inch wide strips. Set aside.

2 In a small bowl, mix together the soy sauce, sherry, sesame oil, sugar, and salt. Set aside. Heat a large wok or skillet over high heat. Add the oil and tilt to coat the inside of the pan. Add the scallions and garlic and stir-fry until fragrant, about 15 seconds. Add the cabbage, carrot, bamboo shoots, and water chestnuts and stir-fry until the cabbage wilts, about 3 minutes. Stir the soy sauce mixture into the vegetables and mix well. Transfer to a shallow dish and let cool completely. Sprinkle with the cornstarch and toss until the vegetables absorb the cornstarch.

3 Preheat the oven to 200°F. Line a baking sheet with waxed paper. Place an egg roll wrapper on a work surface, with the points at 12, 3, 6, and 9 o'clock. Place one sixth of the filling on the bottom third of the wrapper, forming it into a log that comes no closer than 1/2 inch to the edges of the wrapper. Fold up the bottom point, and roll up the wrapper, folding in the side points as you roll it into a thick cylinder. Place a dab of water on the last point to adhere it to the roll. Place the roll, seam-side down, on the waxed paper. Repeat with the remaining filling and wrappers.

continued ➥

6 large dried shiitake mushrooms
1 tablespoon Japanese soy sauce
1 tablespoon dry sherry
2 teaspoons Asian dark sesame oil
1/2 teaspoon sugar
1/4 teaspoon salt
2 tablespoons vegetable oil
1/2 cup chopped scallions, including
    white and green parts
2 garlic cloves, minced
3 cups shredded napa cabbage
1 medium carrot, peeled and cut into
    very thin strips about 2 inches
    long and 1/16 inch wide
1/2 cup canned bamboo shoots,
    rinsed, drained, and thinly
    shredded
1/3 cup canned water chestnuts,
    rinsed, drained, and thinly
    shredded
1 tablespoon cornstarch
6 egg roll wrappers
Vegetable shortening or oil for
    deep-frying
Hoisin sauce, hot Chinese mustard,
    and duck sauce for dipping

Look for egg roll wrappers in the refrigerated section of an Asian grocery. The fewer ingredients and preservatives, the better the wrapper.

4 Place a large wire cake rack over a jelly roll pan. In a deep Dutch oven, melt vegetable shortening over high heat to a depth of 2 to 3 inches and heat it to 365°F. In batches, without crowding, deep-fry the egg rolls until golden brown, about 3 minutes. Using a wire-mesh skimmer, transfer to the wire rack and keep warm in the oven while deep-frying the remaining egg rolls. Serve immediately, with small bowls of the hoisin sauce, mustard, and duck sauce, for dipping.

MAKES 6 LARGE EGG ROLLS

Goat Cheese Wontons
with Tomato-Herb Salsa

Fried wontons are finger food of the highest order, but if you're serving them at a cocktail party, provide plenty of cocktail napkins—the salsa can drip. I serve them most often as a first course, with 6 wontons surrounding a pool of salsa.

1 To make the salsa: In a food processor, pulse all of the ingredients until pureed. Cover and refrigerate until ready to serve, up to 4 hours.

2 To make the wontons: Line a baking sheet with waxed paper. In a medium bowl, mash the goat cheese, bread crumbs, garlic, and pepper with a rubber spatula until combined. Place a wonton wrapper on a work surface, with the points at 12, 3, 6, and 9 o'clock. Brush the edges of a wonton wrapper with cold water. Place 1 teaspoon goat cheese mixture on the bottom third of the wrapper. Fold over the top point of the wrapper to meet the bottom point, enclosing the filling in a triangle shape. Press the edges of the wrapper to seal. Place on the waxed paper. Repeat with the remaining filling and wrappers. (The wontons can be prepared up to 4 hours ahead, covered, and refrigerated.)

3 Preheat the oven to 200°F. Line a baking sheet with paper towels. In a deep Dutch oven, melt vegetable shortening to a depth of 2 to 3 inches and heat it to 365°F. In batches, without crowding, deep-fry the wontons, turning once, until golden brown, about $1\frac{1}{2}$ minutes. Keep the wontons warm in the oven while frying the rest. Using a wire-mesh skimmer, transfer to the paper towels to drain. Serve warm, with the salsa.

MAKES ABOUT 36 WONTONS

Tomato-Herb Salsa

1 pound plum tomatoes, seeded and coarsely chopped
2 tablespoons minced shallots
1 jalapeño chili, seeded and minced
2 teaspoons red wine vinegar
1 garlic clove, crushed through a press
$\frac{1}{4}$ teaspoon salt
2 tablespoons chopped fresh cilantro or basil

Goat Cheese Wontons

8 ounces rindless goat cheese (chèvre) at room temperature
2 tablespoons dried bread crumbs
1 garlic clove, crushed through a press
$\frac{1}{4}$ teaspoon freshly ground pepper
36 wonton wrappers
Vegetable shortening or oil for deep-frying

Fried Dough Knots
with Garlic Oil

¼ cup extra-virgin olive oil
2 garlic cloves, minced
1½ teaspoons active dry yeast
¼ cup warm (105° to 115°F) water
3 cups unbleached flour
¾ teaspoon salt
¾ cup cold water
Vegetable shortening or oil for
    deep-frying

In New York, you can't have a street fair or block party without a fried-dough stand. (You also need a cannoli stand, a funnel cake stand, a French fries stand, and a few other fried-food concessions.) And fried dough knots are found at pizzerias from Boston to Philadelphia as well. These ropes of pizza dough, tied into knots and deep-fried, originated as a garlic oil–slathered snack, but I serve them as the ultimate garlic bread to accompany spaghetti with meat sauce.

1 In a small saucepan, heat the oil and garlic over low heat until tiny bubbles appear around the garlic, about 2 minutes. Remove from heat and let stand at room temperature while preparing the dough knots.

2 In a small bowl, sprinkle the yeast over the warm water and let stand until creamy, about 5 minutes. Stir to dissolve the yeast.

3 In a food processor, pulse the flour and salt to combine. With the machine running, add the yeast mixture and enough cold water to form a ball of dough on top of the blade (there may be smaller particles of dough in the bowl as well as the large ball). If the dough is too wet or too dry, it will not form a ball. Feel the dough, and if it is sticky and wet, add additional flour, 2 tablespoons at a time, processing after each addition, until the dough forms a ball. If it seems too dry, follow the same procedure, adding additional water, 1 tablespoon at a time. Process the ball of dough for 45 seconds. To make the dough by hand, put the flour and salt in a large bowl. Stir in the yeast mixture and stir in enough water to form a shaggy dough. Turn out onto a lightly floured surface and knead until smooth and elastic, about 10 minutes.

4 Lightly grease a medium bowl with shortening. Gather the dough into a ball and place in the bowl, turning the dough to coat it with the shortening. Cover the bowl with plastic wrap and let the dough rise in a warm place until almost doubled, or until a finger, inserted

$\frac{1}{2}$ inch into the dough, leaves an impression, about $1\frac{1}{2}$ hours. Divide the dough into 16 portions and roll into balls. Cover the balls loosely with plastic wrap.

5 Place 1 portion of dough on an unfloured work surface. Roll the dough underneath your hands on the work surface, moving your hands apart in a horizontal movement as you roll, until the dough is rolled and stretched into an 8-inch rope. Pulling and twisting the dough as needed, tie into an overhand knot. Set aside on a floured surface and cover loosely with plastic wrap. Repeat with the remaining dough.

6 Preheat the oven to 200°F. Line a baking sheet with paper towels. In a deep Dutch oven, melt vegetable shortening over high heat to a depth of 2 to 3 inches and heat it to 375°F. In batches, without crowding, deep-fry the dough knots, turning once, until golden brown, about 3 minutes. Using a wire-mesh skimmer, transfer to the paper towels to drain. Keep the knots warm in the oven while frying the rest. Just before serving, brush the dough knots generously with the garlic oil. (The dough knots can be prepared up to 4 hours ahead and stored at room temperature, but they are best served warm.)

MAKES 16 KNOTS

Crab Spring Rolls

Though they use the same kind of wrapper, Thai spring rolls are thinner than Chinese egg rolls and have a filling with classic Southeast Asian ingredients such as bean thread noodles (also called *sai fun*, or cellophane noodles), shallots, cilantro, and fish sauce.

1 To make the sauce: In a small saucepan, mix the vinegar, sugar, water, garlic, and chili paste together. Bring to a simmer over medium heat, stirring to dissolve the sugar. Remove from heat and let stand until cool. (The sauce can be prepared up to 1 day ahead and stored at room temperature.)

2 To make the spring rolls: In a medium bowl, cover the noodles with very hot water. Let stand until the noodles are soft and supple, about 10 minutes. Drain well in a sieve. Using kitchen scissors, snip through the bean threads in the sieve to cut them into more manageable lengths. Place in a bowl, cover with plastic wrap, and set aside.

3 Heat a large wok or skillet over high heat. Add the oil and tilt to coat the inside of the pan. Add the shallots and garlic and stir-fry until fragrant, about 15 seconds. Add the carrot and stir-fry until crisp-tender, about 1 minute. Add the crab, bean sprouts, cilantro, fish sauce, sugar, and chili or Tabasco sauce and stir-fry until heated through, about 2 minutes. Remove from heat and place in a shallow dish. Stir in the bean threads. Let cool completely.

4 Preheat the oven to 200°F. Line a baking sheet with waxed paper. Place an egg roll wrapper on a work surface, with the points at 12, 3, 6, and 9 o'clock. Place about $\frac{1}{4}$ cup filling on the bottom third of the wrapper and form it into a log that comes no closer than $\frac{1}{2}$ inch to the edges of the wrapper. Fold up the bottom point and roll up the egg roll, folding in the side points as you roll it into a tight cylinder. Place a dab of water on the last point to adhere it to the roll. Place the spring roll, seam-side down, on the waxed paper. Repeat with the remaining filling and wrappers.

continued ➤➤

Sweet Garlic Sauce
$\frac{1}{2}$ cup rice vinegar
$\frac{1}{2}$ cup sugar
$\frac{1}{4}$ cup water
3 garlic cloves, thinly sliced
$\frac{1}{2}$ teaspoon Chinese chili
    paste with garlic

Crab Spring Rolls
1 skein (about 2 ounces) bean thread
    noodles
1 tablespoon vegetable oil
$\frac{1}{3}$ cup finely chopped shallots
1 garlic clove, crushed through a
    press
1 medium carrot, peeled and cut into
    2-inch-long matchsticks
8 ounces fresh lump crabmeat, flaked
    and picked over for cartilage
1 cup coarsely chopped bean sprouts
    (about 4 ounces)
$\frac{1}{4}$ cup chopped fresh cilantro
    sprigs with stems
2 tablespoons Asian fish sauce
    (nam pla or nuoc mam)
1 teaspoon sugar
$\frac{1}{4}$ teaspoon Vietnamese hot chili
    sauce or Tabasco sauce
15 egg roll wrappers
Vegetable shortening or oil for
    deep-frying

Vietnamese or Thai fish sauces can be found in Asian groceries. Do not confuse them with Filipino fish sauce (*pastis*), which is lighter in flavor. If necessary, combine 1 teaspoon each Worcestershire sauce, Japanese soy sauce, and water to substitute for each tablespoon of fish sauce.

5 Place a large wire cake rack over a jelly roll pan. In a deep Dutch oven, heat vegetable shortening over high heat to a depth of 2 to 3 inches and heat it to 365°F. In batches, without crowding, deep-fry the spring rolls until golden brown, about 3 minutes. Using a wire-mesh skimmer, transfer to the wire rack and keep warm in the oven while deep-frying the remaining spring rolls. Serve immediately, with small bowls of the garlic sauce for dipping.

MAKES 15 THIN SPRING ROLLS

Beef and Cabbage Piroshki

I developed a fondness for piroshki when I lived in San Francisco's Richmond District, the heart of the city's Russian émigré community. One day, I got the nerve to ask my neighbor Anya for her fine beef-and-cabbage piroshki recipe. Anya was a practical woman, but I didn't realize just how practical until she revealed the secret to her excellent crust: refrigerated biscuits! I've made piroshki her way ever since.

1 To make the filling: In a medium saucepan of lightly salted boiling water, cook the cabbage until tender, about 8 minutes. Drain and rinse under cold running water. A handful at a time, squeeze the excess water from the cabbage. Set aside.

2 In a large skillet over medium heat, heat the oil. Add the onion and garlic and cook until softened, about 3 minutes. Add the ground round and cook, stirring often and breaking up the meat with a spoon, until it loses its pink color, about 5 minutes. Stir in the reserved cabbage and the dill, salt, and pepper, and cook for 2 minutes. Remove from heat and let cool. Stir in the sour cream and egg yolk.

3 Line a baking sheet with a clean kitchen towel. On a lightly floured work surface, roll 1 biscuit into a 3½-inch round. Place about 1 tablespoon of the cooled filling onto the bottom half of the round. Brush the edges with the yolk mixture, fold over to enclose the filling, and press the edges firmly to seal. Place on the kitchen towel and cover loosely with plastic wrap. Repeat with the remaining dough and filling.

4 Line a baking sheet with paper towels. In a deep Dutch oven, melt vegetable shortening over high heat to a depth of 2 to 3 inches and heat it to 350°F. In batches, without crowding, deep-fry the piroshki until golden brown, about 3 minutes. Using a wire-mesh skimmer, transfer to the paper towels to drain. Serve warm.

MAKES 40 PIROSHKI

Beef and Cabbage Filling

3½ cups thinly shredded
    green cabbage
1 tablespoon vegetable oil
1 medium onion, finely chopped
1 garlic clove, crushed through
    a press
1 pound ground round (15 percent fat)
1 tablespoon finely chopped fresh dill
1 teaspoon salt
½ teaspoon freshly ground pepper
3 tablespoons sour cream
1 large egg yolk

Four 7½-ounce cans refrigerated
    buttermilk biscuits
1 large egg yolk beaten with
    1 teaspoon water
Vegetable shortening or oil for
    deep-frying

large fry

main courses

Double-Cooked Fried Chicken 58 • Mo' Betta Fried Chicken 60 •
Italian Fried Chicken 61 • General Tso's Chicken 62 • Two-Tone Buffalo Wings with Blue
Cheese Dip 64 • Turkey Cutlets Parmigiano 66 • Chicken Kiev with Fresh Herbs and Lemon 67
• Deep-Fried Cornish Game Hens 68 • Chicken-Fried Steak with Chipotle Gravy 70 • Crispy
Japanese Pork Cutlets 71 • Chicken Flautas with Orange and Red Onion Salsa 72 • Norman's
Special Garlic Spareribs 74 • Pork and Black Bean Chimichangas 76 • Crispy Oysters with
Rémoulade Cabbage and Corn Slaw 78 • Flounder Fillets with Orange Sweet and Sour
Sauce 80 • Pork and Mushroom Chow Mein 82 • Calamari Fritti with Garlic Mayonnaise 84 •
Delmarva Crab Cakes with Cucumber Tartar Sauce 86

Double-Cooked Fried Chicken

One 4-pound chicken
2 cups buttermilk
1 tablespoon hot red pepper sauce,
    such as Tabasco
1½ cups all-purpose flour
1 teaspoon salt
½ teaspoon freshly ground pepper
Vegetable shortening or oil for
    deep-frying

Traditionalists may disagree, but there's more than one way to fry a chicken. My method fries the chicken to form the delicious crust, then bakes it on a wire rack to give grease-free, evenly cooked, perfect final results. Simple ingredients make the best chicken: a tangy buttermilk and hot sauce marinade, and flour, salt, and pepper for the coating. (It's a waste to season the chicken flour with lots of herbs and spices, because they will only scorch and lose their flavor when deep-fried.)

1 Using a sharp knife, cut the bird into 8 pieces, leaving about one third of the breast attached to each wing so the wing portion will be more substantial. Rinse the chicken and pat dry with paper towels.

2 In a large bowl, combine the buttermilk and hot pepper sauce. Add the chicken and mix well. Cover and refrigerate, stirring the chicken occasionally, for at least 2 hours or up to 24 hours.

3 Drain the chicken. Mix the flour, salt, and pepper in a large paper bag or large bowl. A few pieces at a time, toss the chicken in the flour mixture to coat. Place on waxed paper and let stand for 15 minutes at room temperature to set the coating.

4 Preheat the oven to 350°F. Place a large wire cake rack over a jelly roll pan. In a deep, large skillet, melt vegetable shortening to a depth of 2 to 3 inches and heat it to 375° F. Add the chicken and deep-fry, turning once, until golden brown on both sides, about 12 minutes. Transfer to the wire racks and bake until the chicken shows no sign of pink when pierced at the bone, about 15 minutes. Serve hot or at room temperature. (Fried chicken is best served within 2 hours of frying, and shouldn't be refrigerated, as refrigeration gives the chicken breasts a cottony texture.)

MAKES 4 SERVINGS

Mo' Betta Fried Chicken

3 pounds chicken thighs
1/4 cup dark rum
1/4 cup Japanese soy sauce
1/4 cup fresh lime juice
2 tablespoons packed light brown
    sugar
2 scallions, white and green parts,
    finely chopped
1 Scotch bonnet, serrano, or
    jalapeño chili, seeded and
    minced
1 tablespoon shredded fresh ginger
    (use the large holes of a box
    grater)
1 teaspoon dried thyme
1/4 teaspoon ground allspice
2 garlic cloves, minced
Vegetable shortening or oil for
    deep-frying

Why do I specify Japanese soy sauce in these recipes? Chinese soy sauce, available at Asian grocers, varies greatly in saltiness, quality, and flavor intensity from brand to brand. But Japanese brands, like the familiar Kikkoman found in every supermarket, are more reliable and not as intensely salty. You may use the reduced-sodium variety, if you prefer, but the flavor is weaker than the regular variety.

Just as Americans love crusty fried chicken, Caribbeans love their marinated, crustless version. For the most succulent results, use chicken thighs chopped through the bone into chunky pieces. The spicy marinade of dark rum, soy sauce, and lime juice caramelizes during deep-frying to give the chicken a dark brown coating. Use the Scotch bonnet chili if you love hot foods. Try serving this dish with baked sweet potatoes.

1 Using a heavy cleaver, cut each chicken thigh in half though the bone (or have the butcher do this for you). Rinse the chicken and pat dry with paper towels.

2 In a large bowl or self-sealing plastic bag, mix the rum, soy sauce, lime juice, brown sugar, scallions, chili, ginger, thyme, allspice, and garlic, stirring to dissolve the sugar. Add the chicken and toss well. Cover and refrigerate, turning the chicken occasionally, for at least 2 hours or up to 24 hours.

3 Preheat the oven to 200°F. Place a large wire rack over a jelly roll pan. In a deep Dutch oven, melt shortening over high heat to a depth of 2 to 3 inches and heat it to 365°F. Scrape the marinade solids from the chicken. In batches, without crowding, deep-fry the chicken until the outside is a deep, caramelized brown and the chicken shows no sign of pink when pierced at the bone, about 10 minutes (remove a thigh from the oil to check doneness). Transfer to the wire racks and keep warm in the oven while frying the remaining chicken.

MAKES 4 SERVINGS

Italian Fried Chicken

The Italian version of fried chicken is typical of that cuisine: Uncomplicated and straightforward, it allows the flavors of the ingredients to shine. Like all Italian deep-fried foods, it is especially wonderful when fried in olive oil. Serve with a simple lettuce and tomato salad and steamed asparagus or broccoli, the way I had it in Venice.

1 In a medium bowl, toss the chicken pieces with the lemon juice, oregano, and garlic. Cover and refrigerate for 1 hour.

2 Preheat the oven to 200°F. Place a large wire cake rack over a jelly roll pan. Pour 2 to 3 inches of oil into a deep Dutch oven and heat it to 350°F over high heat.

3 Meanwhile, in a medium bowl, beat the eggs. In a shallow bowl, combine the flour, salt, and pepper and mix well. Working in batches, coat a few chicken pieces with the eggs, then roll in the flour mixture. Deep-fry the chicken until golden brown, turning occasionally, about 4 minutes. Using a wire-mesh skimmer, transfer to the wire rack and keep warm in the oven while frying the rest of the chicken. Serve immediately, with the lemon wedges.

MAKES 4 TO 6 SERVINGS

2 pounds boneless, skinless chicken breasts and thighs, cut into 1-inch pieces
2 tablespoons fresh lemon juice
1½ teaspoons dried oregano
2 garlic cloves, crushed through a press
3 large eggs
1 cup all-purpose flour
½ teaspoon salt
¼ teaspoon freshly ground pepper
Olive oil or vegetable oil for deep-frying
Lemon wedges for serving

General Tso's Chicken

1 pound boneless, skinless chicken
 thighs, cut into 1-inch pieces
1 tablespoon Japanese soy sauce
1 tablespoon dry sherry
1 large egg, beaten
$\frac{1}{2}$ cup cornstarch
3 cups broccoli florets
Peanut, corn, or vegetable oil for
 deep-frying
$\frac{1}{4}$ cup homemade or low-salt canned
 chicken broth
$\frac{1}{4}$ cup Japanese soy sauce
3 tablespoons dry sherry
$\frac{1}{4}$ cup sugar
$1\frac{1}{2}$ tablespoons rice vinegar
1 tablespoon cornstarch
6 tablespoons cold water
1 tablespoon minced garlic
10 small whole dried red chilies

Whenever I have a question about the intricacies of Chinese cuisine, I make a call to my friend, Norman Weinstein, one of the East Coast's best cooking teachers. I wanted to know how to make my favorite Chinese dish, General Tso's chicken, and Norman came through with this absolutely terrific recipe that runs circles around whatever you can order from your neighborhood takeout. This was supposedly invented by a famous Hunan general before a big battle. Whoever the inventor was, he or she discovered that three successive dips in oil produces the very crisp crust that makes this a deep-fried classic. (Just try to get that golden crust in an oven!)

1 At least 1 hour before serving, coat the chicken: Place a large wire cake rack over a jelly roll pan. Place the chicken in a medium bowl. Add the soy sauce and sherry and mix well. Add the egg and mix again until well coated. Put the $\frac{1}{2}$ cup cornstarch in a shallow bowl. A few pieces at a time, roll the chicken in the cornstarch. Place on the wire rack without the pieces touching each other. Set the bowl of cornstarch aside. Cover the chicken loosely with plastic wrap and refrigerate to set the coating, at least 30 minutes or up to 4 hours, the longer the better. Remove from the refrigerator 30 minutes before deep-frying.

2 In a large saucepan of lightly salted boiling water, cook the broccoli to set the color, about 1 minute. Using a wire-mesh skimmer, transfer the broccoli to a bowl of cold water and set aside. Keep the water boiling.

3 Heat a large flat-bottomed wok or deep Dutch oven over high heat until very hot. Add enough oil to come about one third of the way up the sides of the wok or to a depth of 2 to 3 inches in the Dutch oven. Over high heat, heat the oil until very hot, but not smoking (the surface of the oil will shimmer slightly), or to 400°F on a deep-frying thermometer.

4 In a small bowl, combine the broth, soy sauce, sherry, sugar, and vinegar, stirring to dissolve the sugar as much as possible. In another small bowl, dissolve the remaining 1 tablespoon cornstarch in the water.

5 Roll the chicken again in the bowl of cornstarch. In batches, without crowding, deep-fry the chicken pieces until the coating sets, about 30 seconds. Using a wire-mesh skimmer, remove the chicken and count to 10. Return the chicken to the oil and cook until golden, about 15 seconds. Remove from the oil, count to 10, and deep-fry a third time until the coating is crisp and golden brown, about 1 minute. Transfer to a platter and set aside while deep-frying the remaining chicken.

6 Pour off all but 2 tablespoons of the oil from the wok. Return to high heat and add the chilies. Cook until the chilies are dark red (the longer they cook, the darker they get and the spicier the dish, so adjust the cooking time according to taste). Stir the soy sauce mixture into the wok, then stir in the garlic. Reduce heat to low and simmer for 20 seconds. Add the cornstarch mixture and stir until thickened. Add the chicken pieces and stir to coat them with the sauce. Transfer to the center of a platter. Drain the broccoli from the bowl of water and return the broccoli to the saucepan of boiling water. Cook just until heated through, about 30 seconds. Drain and arrange the broccoli around the chicken. Serve immediately.

MAKES 4 SERVINGS

Two-Tone Buffalo Wings

When in Buffalo, food-lovers make a pilgrimage to the Anchor Bar, home of the original Buffalo wings. A lot of people eat wings as an appetizer, but they make a good meal, too. The secret to good wings is the kind of hot sauce used for the coating. All hot sauces are not alike. Tabasco is very hot and vinegary, whereas Durkee (which is rumored to be the Anchor's preferred brand) is much milder. With so many hot sauces now available, I make at least two different coatings. One is red, made from from a reasonably mellow Louisiana brand, such as Frank's or Crystal. The green wings come from a jalapeño-based sauce (Tabasco makes one, but there are also fun, fiery Mexican varieties in strange bottles).

1 To make the dip: In a medium bowl, combine the mayonnaise, sour cream, blue cheese, milk, lemon juice, celery seed, and pepper. Cover and refrigerate for at least 1 hour or up to 24 hours before serving.

2 To make the Buffalo wings: Using a heavy cleaver, chop each wing between the joints to make 3 pieces. Discard the wing tips (or save for another use, such as making chicken stock). If desired, ask the butcher to do this for you, or purchase precut chicken wings. Let the wings stand at room temperature for 30 minutes before frying.

3 Meanwhile, in a small saucepan, melt the butter with the garlic over low heat. Divide the garlic butter between 2 large bowls. Add the red hot sauce to one bowl and whisk well to combine. Add the green hot sauce to the other bowl and whisk. Set the bowls aside.

4 Preheat the oven to 200°F. Put a large wire cake rack over a jelly roll pan. In a deep Dutch oven, melt shortening over high heat to a depth of 2 to 3 inches and heat it to 365°F. In batches, without crowding, deep-fry the chicken wings until they are golden brown and show no sign of pink when pierced at the bone (remove a wing from the fat to check the doneness), about 3 minutes. Using a wire-mesh skimmer, transfer the wings to the racks and keep warm in the oven while frying the remaining wings.

5 Add half the wings to each bowl of sauce and toss well to coat. Serve the coated wings immediately, with the blue cheese sauce on the side for dipping and an empty bowl to collect the bones.

Makes 4 servings

Blue Cheese Dip

½ cup mayonnaise
½ cup sour cream
½ cup crumbled blue cheese
3 tablespoons milk
1 tablespoon fresh lemon juice
½ teaspoon celery seed
¼ teaspoon freshly ground pepper

Two-Tone Buffalo Wings

4 pounds chicken wings
½ cup (1 stick) unsalted butter
2 garlic cloves, crushed
    through a press
3 tablespoons hot red pepper sauce,
    or to taste
2 tablespoons hot green jalapeño
    sauce, or to taste
Vegetable shortening or oil for
    deep-frying

Buffalo wings have become so popular that the precut wings can be purchased in 3- to 10-pound bags at price clubs and many supermarkets.

Turkey Cutlets Parmigiano

Four 5-ounce turkey cutlets
½ cup (2 ounces) freshly grated
    Parmigiano-Reggiano cheese
3 large eggs
1 tablespoon finely chopped rosemary
½ teaspoon salt
¼ teaspoon freshly ground pepper
2 cups fresh bread crumbs, preferably
    made from day-old bread
Olive oil for frying
Lemon wedges for serving

Northern Italy uses turkey in many recipes, sometimes as a substitute for veal. Here, turkey cutlets are dipped in freshly grated Parmigiano-Reggiano, then breaded and fried to perfection in olive oil. Like most Italian recipes, it isn't complicated, but it does depend on good ingredients. Be sure to use true Parmigiano, not one of the many cheeses out there labeled "Parmesan" that aren't from Italy.

1 Rinse the turkey cutlets under cold water and shake off the excess water. Put the cheese in a shallow bowl. In another shallow bowl, beat the eggs, rosemary, salt, and pepper. Put the bread crumbs in a third shallow bowl.

2 Line a baking sheet with waxed paper. One at a time, dip the turkey cutlets in the cheese, patting to help it adhere. Dip the cutlets in the egg mixture, then into the bread crumbs. Set aside.

3 Place a large wire cake rack over a jelly roll pan. Into a deep, heavy skillet (preferably cast iron), pour 1 inch olive oil and heat it over medium-high heat until very hot, but not smoking. Fry the cutlets, turning once, just until golden brown, about 6 to 7 minutes. Using a slotted spoon, transfer to the wire rack to drain briefly. Serve immediately, with the lemon wedges.

MAKES 4 SERVINGS

Chicken Kiev *with Fresh Herbs and Lemon*

Chicken Kiev is a surefire dinner entree. It was one of the first "fancy" dishes I taught myself how to cook from a cookbook by Michael Field (a food professional who died before the gourmet craze really took off, and who is vastly underappreciated).

1 Using a small, sharp knife, with the tip of the knife pointing towards the bones, remove the thin rib bones and thick keel bone from each breast, keeping the breast meat and skin intact. (Or ask the butcher to do this for you.) Using a flat meat mallet, pound the breasts lightly so they are the same thickness throughout. Sprinkle with the lemon juice and season with the salt and pepper. Cover and refrigerate until the butter is ready.

2 In a medium bowl, using a rubber spatula, cream the butter and blend in the chives, tarragon, rosemary, thyme, zest, salt, and pepper. The butter should be just malleable. If it is too soft, place in the freezer to firm. Form the butter into 6 equal finger-shaped pieces about 3 inches long.

3 Using a sharp knife, cut a deep horizontal slit into the side of each breast. Insert a butter finger into each slit, and press the edges of the slit closed to seal.

4 Put the flour in a deep plate. Break the eggs into a second plate and beat well. Place the bread crumbs in a third plate. Coat each breast first with flour, then with eggs, then bread crumbs. Place on a baking sheet and refrigerate for at least 30 minutes or up to 4 hours to set the crumbs.

5 Put a large wire cake rack over a jelly roll pan. In a large, deep skillet, melt vegetable shortening over high heat to a depth of 2 to 3 inches and heat it to 360°F. Carefully place the breasts in the hot shortening and deep-fry for 5 minutes. Turn carefully and continue cooking until the breasts are golden brown, about 3 to 5 minutes. Using tongs, transfer to the wire rack to drain briefly. Serve immediately, warning each guest that the butter may squirt out of the chicken breast when pierced.

MAKES 4 SERVINGS

4 bone-in chicken breast halves
(11 to 13 ounces each)
¼ teaspoon salt
¼ teaspoon freshly ground pepper
2 tablespoons fresh lemon juice
6 tablespoons unsalted butter at cool
room temperature
1 tablespoon finely chopped fresh
chives
1 teaspoon finely chopped fresh
tarragon
1 teaspoon finely chopped fresh
rosemary
1 teaspoon finely chopped fresh
thyme
Grated zest of 1 lemon
⅛ teaspoon salt
⅛ teaspoon freshly ground pepper

½ cup all-purpose flour
3 large eggs
1½ cups fresh bread crumbs, preferably made from day-old bread
Vegetable shortening or oil for
deep-frying

Deep-Fried Cornish Game Hens

Two 1½-pound Cornish game hens
Vegetable shortening or oil for
 deep-frying
Salt, freshly ground pepper, and
 lemon wedges for serving

Some folks like to deep-fry a whole turkey—I'll admit it's good, but what a hassle! First, you have to locate a huge stockpot, an outdoor propane gas burner large enough to hold it, and enough oil to fill the pot by half. It's also very dangerous (ever try to lift a 20-pound turkey out of boiling fat?). However, the method is good enough to apply in more sensible proportions to Cornish game hens. These can be done indoors, but there are still precautions. First, don't fill your stockpot more than half full with shortening, to allow for the inevitable boiling up when the hens are added. Also, be sure the hens are at room temperature so the fat temperature doesn't drop dramatically from the shock of an ice-cold bird. If you like juicy, golden, crispy poultry that is so good it needs no more than a squirt of lemon juice and a sprinkle of salt and pepper, get to know this technique.

1 Rinse the hens and pat completely dry, inside and out, with paper towels. Let stand at room temperature for 1 hour.

2 Preheat the oven to 200°F. Place a large wire cake rack over a jelly roll pan. In a stockpot, melt vegetable shortening over high heat to a depth of 2 to 3 inches and heat it to 375°F. Carefully put 1 Cornish hen in the hot shortening. Deep-fry, turning occasionally, until golden brown, about 12 minutes. To check for doneness, using a wire-mesh skimmer and tongs, carefully remove the hen from the stockpot and insert an instant-read thermometer in the thickest part of the thigh, not touching a bone—it should read 180°F. Transfer to the wire rack and keep warm in the oven while frying the other hen. Let the second hen rest for 5 minutes. Serve whole, or use a cleaver to split the hens lengthwise. Serve with the salt, pepper, and lemon wedges, letting each person season his or her hen to taste.

MAKES 2 TO 4 SERVINGS

Chicken-Fried Steak
with Chipotle Gravy

1 pound ½-inch-thick top round
   steak, trimmed and cut into 4
   equal pieces
Vegetable shortening or oil for
   deep-frying
1 cup buttermilk
1 teaspoon hot red pepper sauce,
   such as Tabasco
1 cup all-purpose flour
1 teaspoon salt, plus salt to taste
½ teaspoon freshly ground pepper
2 cups milk
1 canned chipotle en adobo, finely
   chopped, with any clinging sauce

Chicken-fried steak, like many other humble dishes, is a clever way to improve a not-so-tender cut of meat. Pounding round steak makes it tender, and the crisp coating protects the meat from drying out. A bit of chipotle chili adds some kick to the traditional milk gravy—substitute any hot red pepper sauce if chipotle isn't available. Don't forget to make lots of mashed potatoes for the gravy!

1 Using the pointed side of a meat mallet, pound the steaks to tenderize them. Then use the flat side of the mallet to pound the steaks ¼ inch thick.

2 Preheat the oven to 200°F. Place a large wire rack over a jelly roll pan. In a deep, heavy skillet (preferably cast iron), melt shortening over high heat to a depth of 2 to 3 inches and heat it to 375°F.

3 In a shallow bowl, mix the buttermilk and hot pepper sauce. In another shallow bowl, combine the flour, 1 teaspoon salt, and the pepper and mix well. Dip each steak in the buttermilk, then the flour mixture. Reserve 1½ tablespoons of the flour mixture and set aside. Two at a time, deep-fry the steaks, turning once, until golden brown on both sides, about 3 minutes. Using a slotted spatula, transfer to the wire rack and keep warm in the oven while making the gravy.

4 Discard all but 1½ tablespoons of the shortening from the skillet. Over low heat, whisk in the reserved flour mixture. Let bubble for 1 minute. Whisk in the milk and chipotle and bring to a simmer. Simmer until no trace of flour taste remains, about 3 minutes. Season with salt to taste. Serve the steak immediately, with the gravy.

MAKES 4 SERVINGS

Crispy Japanese Pork Cutlets

Known in Japan as *tonkatsu*, **these breaded cutlets are as popular there as hamburgers are here. The cutlets are usually sliced to facilitate eating with chopsticks, and are served on shredded cabbage, which is heated by the pork's juices. (I add other vegetables to the cabbage and hot rice to round out the meal.) The pork is dipped in thick, somewhat sweet tonkatsu sauce, which can be found at the same Asian grocers that sell panko, or you can make your own. Panko are fluffy Japanese bread crumb flakes that give food an especially light coating; substitute bread crumbs made from slightly stale bread, if you wish.**

1 Preheat the oven to 200°F. Line a baking sheet with waxed paper. Place a large wire cake rack over a jelly roll pan. Into a deep, heavy skillet (preferably cast iron), pour 1 inch of oil and heat it over high heat until very hot but not smoking.

2 In a shallow bowl, combine the flour, salt, and pepper. In another shallow bowl, beat the eggs well. In a third shallow bowl, put the panko. Working with 2 cutlets at a time, coat each cutlet with the flour mixture, then the eggs, then the panko. Place on the waxed paper. Deep-fry 2 cutlets, turning once, until golden brown, about 3 minutes. Transfer to the wire rack to drain and keep warm in the oven while frying the other 2 cutlets.

3 To serve, in a medium bowl, mix the cabbage, carrots, and scallions. Divide the vegetable mixture evenly among 4 dinner plates. Cut each cutlet lengthwise into 3/4-inch-thick slices and arrange each sliced cutlet over the vegetables. Serve immediately, with the lemon wedges and a small bowl of tonkatsu sauce for each guest to dip the pork.

MAKES 4 SERVINGS

Tonkatsu Sauce: In a small bowl, mix 2/3 cup apple butter, 2 tablespoons Japanese soy sauce, 2 tablespoons ketchup, and 1 teaspoon Worcestershire sauce. Makes about 1 cup.

Vegetable oil for deep-frying
1/4 cup all-purpose flour
1/4 teaspoon salt
1/4 teaspoon freshly ground pepper
2 large eggs
1 cup panko (Japanese bread flakes)
Four 4-ounce boneless center-cut
    pork chops, pounded between
    waxed paper until 1/4 inch thick
6 cups thinly shredded napa cabbage
2 medium carrots, peeled and
    shredded
2 scallions, white and green parts,
    finely chopped
Lemon wedges for serving
Tonkatsu Sauce (recipe below) or
    bottled sauce

Chicken Flautas

with Orange and Red Onion Salsa

Chicken Flautas

Two 11-ounce bone-in chicken breast
    halves
1 medium onion, sliced
2 garlic cloves, crushed under a knife
1 teaspoon dried oregano
1 teaspoon cumin seed
½ teaspoon salt
½ teaspoon whole peppercorns
Eight 6-inch corn tortillas

Orange and Red Onion Salsa

2 large navel oranges
1 small red onion, thinly sliced
2 tablespoons chopped fresh cilantro
1 tablespoon fresh lime juice
1 jalapeño chili, sliced into thin
    rounds
1 garlic clove, pressed
⅛ teaspoon salt

½ cup sour cream
3 tablespoons milk
Vegetable shortening or oil for
    deep-frying

Flautas are eaten in Mexico as a snack or light lunch, drizzled with sour cream, but I like them for supper with rice and black beans.

1 To make the flautas: In a medium saucepan, combine the chicken breasts, onion, garlic, oregano, cumin, salt, and peppercorns. Add enough cold water to cover the chicken by 1 inch. Bring to a boil over high heat. Reduce heat to medium-low. Simmer for 20 minutes (the chicken will not be completely cooked). Remove from the heat, cover tightly, and let the chicken cool in the liquid, about 1 hour.

2 Remove the chicken from the bones, shred the chicken, and discard the skin and bones. Set the chicken aside.

3 Heat a dry medium skillet over medium heat. Add a tortilla to the skillet and heat, turning once, until pliable, about 30 seconds. Place on a work surface. Add one eighth of the shredded chicken and roll up the tortilla into a narrow "flute," securing the tortilla closed with a wooden toothpick. Repeat with the remaining tortillas and chicken. (The flautas can be prepared up to 1 hour ahead of frying, covered, and set aside.)

4 Meanwhile, to make the salsa: Using a large knife, cut the top and bottom from each orange down to the flesh. Put the oranges on end and cut off the peel down to the flesh. Cut between the membranes to release the segments. In a medium bowl, combine the orange segments, red onion, cilantro, lime juice, jalapeño, garlic, and salt. Cover and refrigerate until ready to serve, not more than 2 hours.

5 Just before frying the flautas, thin the sour cream with the milk.

6 Preheat the oven to 200°F. Put a large wire cake rack over a jelly roll pan. In 2 batches, in a deep Dutch oven, melt shortening over high heat to a depth of 2 to 3 inches and heat it to 375°F. Deep-fry the flautas until golden brown, about 3 minutes. Using a wire-mesh skimmer, transfer to the wire rack to drain. Keep the flautas warm in the oven while frying the rest.

Serve the flautas on individual plates, drizzled with the sour cream (or use a squeeze bottle to pipe streaks of sour cream over the flautas) and garnished with spoonfuls of the salsa.

MAKES 8 FLAUTAS

Norman's Special Garlic Spareribs

2½ pounds spareribs
2 tablespoons Chinese salted
(sometimes called fermented)
black beans
2 scallions, white and green parts,
finely chopped
1 tablespoon minced garlic
1 tablespoon shredded fresh ginger
(use the large holes of a box
grater)
½ teaspoon hot red pepper flakes
3 tablespoons Japanese soy sauce
1 tablespoon dry sherry
1 tablespoon red wine vinegar
1 tablespoon sugar
2 teaspoons Asian dark sesame oil
½ cup cornstarch
Vegetable oil for deep-frying
Chopped scallion, white and green
parts, for garnish (optional)

It's not just the flavor of the tender spareribs that makes this dish special, but the unusual cooking method that combines deep-frying and steaming. The ribs are cut into bite-sized pieces, a job that should be done by the butcher. The steaming is most efficiently done in an aluminum tiered steamer, available at Asian housewares stores and grocers. Inexpensive bamboo steamers, set over a saucepan of simmering water, will work, but the aluminum ones hold the steam better. A good alternative is to steam the ribs on a large heatproof platter set on a collapsible steamer in a large, covered roasting pan. This is another contribution from my friend and Asian-cooking expert, Norman Weinstein.

1 Have the butcher prepare the spareribs as follows: Remove the chine (back) bone from the rack of ribs and cleave it into bite-sized pieces. Saw the rack horizontally into 1-inch-long strips. Cut between the bones to make bite-sized pieces.

2 In a small bowl, soak the black beans in warm water to cover for 5 minutes. Drain. Return to the bowl and mix with the scallions, garlic, ginger, and hot pepper flakes. In another small bowl, mix the soy sauce, sherry, vinegar, sugar, and sesame oil, stirring to dissolve the sugar. Set aside.

3 Pour enough oil into a large, flat-bottomed wok or deep Dutch oven to come one third to halfway up the sides. Heat over high heat until the oil is very hot, but not smoking (the surface of the oil will shimmer slightly), 375°F on a deep-frying thermometer. Place the cornstarch in a medium bowl. Working with about one half of the ribs at a time, coat the ribs with the cornstarch, shaking off the excess. Deep-fry until the coating is set, about 45 seconds. Using a wire-mesh strainer, transfer the ribs to a platter. Repeat with the remaining ribs.

4 Pour off all but 2 tablespoons oil from the pan. (If too much cornstarch has fallen to the bottom of the oil in the pan, discard the cloudy oil, wipe out the pan with paper towels, and use a new 3 tablespoons oil.) Return to high heat. Add the black bean mixture and stir-fry until fragrant, about 15 seconds. Stir the soy sauce mixture well, and pour into the pan. Add the ribs and stir well to coat with the sauce. Remove from heat. Place the ribs in single layers on round heatproof plates that will fit the steamer tiers with at least 1 inch of empty space around the sides. (You might need 2 or 3 plates, depending on the size of your steamer and the number of tiers.) Pour equal amounts of the sauce over the plates.

5 Fill the bottom of the steamer halfway with water and bring it to a boil over high heat. Reduce heat to medium to maintain a steady boil and a good head of steam. Stack the tiers over the pot and cover with the steamer lid. Steam the ribs, adding more boiling water to the saucepan as needed, until the ribs are tender, about 1 hour.

6 Carefully transfer the ribs and sauce to a serving platter. Serve hot or at room temperature, garnished with the chopped scallion. (The spareribs can be prepared up to 1 day ahead, cooled, covered, and refrigerated. Reheat by steaming again over boiling water until heated through, about 10 minutes.)

MAKES 4 SERVINGS

Pork and Black Bean Chimichangas

2 tablespoons olive oil

One 4½-pound pork shoulder, untrimmed

½ teaspoon salt

1 medium onion, chopped

3 garlic cloves, crushed under a knife

1¾ cups homemade or low-salt canned chicken broth

12 ounces lager beer

2 teaspoons dried oregano

2 imported bay leaves

½ teaspoon whole black peppercorns

1 ripe Hass avocado, pitted, peeled, and coarsely chopped

½ cup sour cream

⅓ cup milk

¼ teaspoon salt

⅛ teaspoon hot red pepper sauce, such as Tabasco

1½ cups cooked black beans, or one 15½-ounce can, drained and rinsed

½ cup bottled salsa, lightly drained to remove excess liquid

Six 9-inch flour tortillas

Vegetable shortening or oil for deep-frying

One of the secrets of Mexican cuisine is shredded long-cooked pork shoulder (also called pork butt, and sometimes labeled pernil or calas). Moist and flavorful, it becomes the filling for many a Mexican specialty, from tacos and burritos to these deep-fried chimichangas. Chimichangas are sometimes described as deep-fried burritos, but the difference is more distinct, as "chimis" have a drier filling—this one is just pork, beans, and salsa. Plan to cook the pork shoulder early in the day, or even the day before.

1 Preheat the oven to 325°F. In a large Dutch oven, heat the oil over high heat. Add the pork shoulder and cook, turning occasionally, until browned on all sides, about 8 minutes. Season with the salt and transfer to a platter.

2 Return the Dutch oven to medium heat and add the onion and garlic. Cook, stirring occasionally, until the onion softens, about 5 minutes. Add the broth, beer, and enough cold water to come two-thirds up the sides of the pork. Bring to a simmer over high heat, skimming off any foam that rises to the surface. Add the oregano, bay leaves, and peppercorns. Cover tightly and place in the oven. Bake, turning the roast halfway through cooking, until the pork is fork-tender, about 3½ hours. Remove from the oven, uncover, and let the pork cool completely in the liquid.

3 Remove the pork from the cooking liquid. Discard the skin, bones, and excess fat. Shred the pork with 2 forks, place in a bowl, and set aside. You should have about 5 cups shredded pork. Reserve 3 cups, saving the remainder for another use. (The pork can be frozen for up to 2 months.)

4 Mash the avocado, sour cream, milk, salt, and hot pepper sauce to make a chunky sauce. Cover and set aside.

5 To assemble the chimichangas, mix the beans and salsa into the shredded pork. In a dry medium skillet over medium heat, heat a tortilla, turning once, until pliable, about 30 seconds. Place on a work surface. Spoon about ½ cup of the filling on the bottom third of the tortilla. Fold up the bottom of the tortilla to cover the filling, fold in the sides, and roll into a thick cylinder. Secure the tortilla closed with a wooden toothpick. Repeat with the remaining tortillas and filling.

6 Preheat the oven to 200°F. Place a large wire cake rack over a jelly roll pan. In a deep Dutch oven, melt vegetable shortening over high heat to a depth of 2 to 3 inches and heat it to 365°F. In batches, without crowding, deep-fry the chimichangas until golden brown, about 3 minutes. Using a wire-mesh skimmer, transfer to the wire rack and keep warm in the oven while frying the rest. Serve hot, with the avocado crema on the side to use as a condiment.

MAKES 6 CHIMICHANGAS

The braised pork shoulder recipe will give you leftovers that freeze beautifully for future meals. Try the pork as a substitute for the shredded chicken in the flautas on page 72.

Crispy Oysters

with Rémoulade Cabbage and Corn Slaw

Rémoulade Cabbage and Corn Slaw

2 cups shredded cabbage

2 cups fresh corn kernels

2 plum tomatoes, seeded and
  chopped

2 scallions, white and green parts,
  chopped

½ cup Garlic Mayonnaise (page 84),
  made with 1 garlic clove

2 tablespoons nonpareil capers,
  rinsed

2 tablespoons finely chopped fresh
  parsley

1 tablespoon Creole or spicy brown
  mustard

¼ teaspoon salt

¼ teaspoon freshly ground pepper

Crispy Oysters

½ cup all-purpose flour

2 teaspoons Bayou Seasoning
  (recipe below)

4 large eggs

1 teaspoon hot red pepper sauce,
  such as Tabasco

1 cup unseasoned dried bread
  crumbs

24 large oysters, such as Blue Points,
  shucked

Vegetable shortening or oil for
  deep-frying

This combination was inspired by the "peacemaker," a New Orleans sandwich stuffed with deep-fried seafood. Without the bread, you can really appreciate the plump oysters in their crispy bread coating. Use somewhat large oysters, such as Blue Points, not small varieties like Olympias, which would get lost in the coating.

1 To make the slaw: In a large bowl, combine all of the slaw ingredients. Cover and refrigerate for at least 2 hours or up to 8 hours.

2 To make the oysters: Line a baking sheet with waxed paper. Place a large wire cake rack over a jelly roll pan. Put the flour and Bayou Seasoning in a shallow bowl. In a medium bowl, beat the eggs and red pepper sauce. In another shallow bowl, spread the bread crumbs. One at a time, coat the oysters with the flour, then the spiced eggs, then the bread crumbs, and place on the waxed paper.

3 Preheat the oven to 200°F. In a deep Dutch oven, melt vegetable shortening over high heat to a depth of 2 to 3 inches and heat it to 350°F. In batches, without crowding, deep-fry the oysters until golden, about 2 minutes. Using a wire-mesh strainer, transfer to the paper towels and keep warm in the oven while frying the remaining oysters.

4 To serve, spoon the slaw on one side of the plate and place the oysters on the other side. Serve immediately.

MAKES 4 SERVINGS

Bayou Seasoning: This mixture is indispensable in Louisiana dishes like gumbo and jambalaya. Mix 2 tablespoons sweet paprika (preferably Hungarian), 1 teaspoon each dried thyme and dried basil, ½ teaspoon each garlic powder, onion powder, and ground pepper, and ¼ teaspoon cayenne pepper. The seasoning will keep indefinitely in a tightly covered container, stored at room temperature in a cool, dark place. Makes about 3 tablespoons.

Flounder Fillets
with Orange Sweet and Sour Sauce

Chinese cooks often serve deep-fried whole fish, but fish fillets are much easier to handle. When served in the traditional style, the dish is called "squirrel fish," because the fish curls up like a squirrel's tail. As in most Asian recipes, the ingredient list looks daunting, but once you get the measuring out of the way, the procedure goes quickly.

1 To make the sauce: In a small bowl, mix all the ingredients except the cornstarch. Add the cornstarch and stir until dissolved. Set aside.

2 In a small bowl, cover the mushrooms with hot water. Let stand until softened, about 30 minutes. Drain. Cut off and discard the tough stems, if attached. Cut each mushroom into quarters.

3 In a medium saucepan of salted boiling water, cook the carrots just until crisp-tender, about 1 minute. Drain and set aside.

4 Place the ginger in a clean kitchen towel. Squeeze and wring the ginger over a bowl to extract the juice. Stir in the soy sauce. Rub the ginger juice mixture into each fillet, and season with the pepper.

5 Preheat the oven to 200°F. Place a large wire cake rack over a jelly roll pan. Heat a large flat-bottomed wok or deep skillet over high heat. Add enough oil to come halfway up the sides and heat it over high heat until very hot, but not smoking (the surface will shimmer slightly), or a deep-frying thermometer reads 375°F.

6 Put the cornstarch in a shallow bowl. Coat each fish fillet with cornstarch. In batches, without crowding, deep-fry the fish fillets until golden brown, about 3 minutes. Using a wire-mesh skimmer, transfer to a wire rack to drain and keep warm in the oven while frying the rest of the fillets. Arrange the fish on a large platter and keep warm in the oven while making the sauce.

7 Pour off all the oil from the wok. Wipe out the cornstarch in the wok with paper towels. Return 2 tablespoons of the oil to the wok and place over high heat. Add the carrots, mushrooms, scallions, and peas, and stir-fry until the scallions begin to wilt, about 30 seconds. Stir the sauce mixture, pour into the wok, and stir until boiling and thickened. Pour the sauce over the fish and serve immediately.

MAKES 4 SERVINGS

Orange Sweet and Sour Sauce

¼ cup homemade or low-salt canned chicken broth
¼ cup fresh orange juice
¼ cup rice vinegar
3 tablespoons ketchup
2 tablespoons packed light brown sugar
1 tablespoon Japanese soy sauce
½ teaspoon chili paste with garlic, or hot red pepper sauce
2 teaspoons cornstarch

6 medium dried shiitake mushrooms
2 medium carrots, peeled and cut into ⅛-inch diagonal slices
2 tablespoons shredded fresh ginger (use the large holes on a box grater)
1 tablespoon soy sauce
Four 4-ounce flounder fillets
¼ teaspoon freshly ground pepper
½ cup cornstarch
Vegetable oil for deep-frying
3 scallions, white and green parts, chopped
½ cup frozen peas, thawed

Dried shiitake mushrooms, sometimes called dried black Chinese mushrooms, are used in many Asian dishes. They have a milder flavor than other dried mushrooms, such as Italian porcini. They range in size from small to very large. In general, the larger mushrooms are the most expensive, but they have the strongest flavor. I use the moderately priced medium-sized shiitakes. They can be purchased at Asian grocers and many supermarkets.

Pork and Mushroom Chow Mein

9 ounces fresh Chinese egg noodles or linguine

3 tablespoons plus ½ cup vegetable oil

1¼ cups low-salt canned beef broth

3 tablespoons Japanese soy sauce

1 tablespoon molasses

1 tablespoon cornstarch

1 pound boneless pork loin, cut into 1-inch pieces

1 large onion, chopped

3 medium celery ribs, cut into ¼-inch diagonal slices

5 ounces fresh mushrooms, sliced

8 ounces fresh bean sprouts, rinsed

On Sunday afternoons, my mom and dad often took us to San Francisco's Chinatown, where we would buy the ingredients to make chow mein for that night's dinner. Dad became a noodle-frying expert, and to this day impresses us when he turns the giant noodle pancake. (Now that I'm a grownup, too, I see that it's not as hard as it looks.) Although new Asian flavors have been introduced to the American palate since the 1960s, this is still a Rodgers family favorite, comforting in its simple flavors of soy sauce, pork, and vegetables, with relative newcomers like fresh ginger, hot chilies, and Asian sesame oil nowhere to be seen.

1 Bring a large pot of salted water to a boil over high heat. Add the noodles and cook until barely tender, about 3 minutes. Drain well and rinse under cold running water. Toss the noodles with 1 tablespoon of the oil.

2 Preheat the oven to 200°F. Line a pizza pan or large baking sheet with paper towels. In a small bowl, combine the broth, soy sauce, and molasses. Add the cornstarch and stir to dissolve. Set aside.

3 In a large (10- to 12-inch) nonstick skillet, heat the ½ cup oil over high heat until very hot, but not smoking. Carefully add the noodles, spreading them in a thick layer. Adjust the heat to medium-high and cook the underside of the noodle pancake until golden brown, about 4 minutes. Using a large, slotted spatula, carefully turn the pancake and brown the other side, about 4 more minutes. Transfer the noodle pancake to the paper towels and keep warm in the oven while preparing the pork and vegetables.

4 Return the skillet to high heat and add 1 tablespoon of the oil. Add the pork and cook, stirring often, until browned on all sides, about 6 minutes. Transfer to a platter and set aside.

5 Add the onion and celery to the skillet and cook, stirring often, until the vegetables soften, about 5 minutes. Stir in the mushrooms and cook until the mushrooms are tender, about 5 minutes. Return the pork to the skillet and cook for 2 minutes. Add the bean sprouts and stir for 1 minute. Stir the soy sauce mixture well. Pour into the skillet and cook until thickened, about 1 minute.

6 Place the noodle pancake on a large, round platter, or cut the pancake into wedges, place the wedges on individual dinner plates, and top with the pork, vegetables, and sauce. Serve immediately.

MAKES 4 TO 6 SERVINGS

Calamari Fritti
with Garlic Mayonnaise

Garlic Mayonnaise

1 large egg at room temperature (see Note)

1 tablespoon fresh lemon juice

1 teaspoon Dijon mustard

2 garlic cloves, crushed through a press

1/4 teaspoon salt

1/8 teaspoon hot red pepper sauce, such as Tabasco

1 cup vegetable oil

1/2 cup extra-virgin olive oil

Calamari Fritti

5 large eggs

1/2 teaspoon salt

1/4 teaspoon freshly ground pepper

1 cup durum semolina (pasta flour) or all-purpose flour

12 ounces squid, cleaned and sacs cut crosswise into 5/16-inch-thick rings, with tentacles left intact

Vegetable oil for deep-frying

While golden rings of calamari are a great appetizer, squid-lovers like me serve them as a main course, too. There are many options for coating squid. You'll get the most tender results with a simple dip in eggs and flour (if you like a crispier coating, try the Ale Batter on page 103). All-purpose flour makes a delicate crust, but semolina provides a gentle crunch. Don't overcook the calamari, or they will toughen.

1 To make the mayonnaise: In a blender, combine the egg, lemon juice, mustard, garlic, salt, and pepper sauce. In a glass measuring cup, combine the vegetable and olive oils. With the machine running, gradually pour the oils through the opening in the lid—it should take about 1 minute—until the mayonnaise thickens. Transfer to a bowl, cover, and refrigerate until ready to serve. (The mayonnaise can be prepared up to 2 days ahead.)

2 To make the calamari: Line a baking sheet with waxed paper. In a medium bowl, beat the eggs, salt, and pepper together. Place the semolina in a shallow bowl. A few at a time, coat the squid pieces with the egg, then roll in the semolina, shaking off the excess. Place on the waxed paper.

3 Preheat the oven to 200°F. Place a large wire cake rack over a jelly roll pan. Pour oil to a depth of 2 to 3 inches into a deep Dutch oven. Over high heat, heat it to 365°F. In batches, without crowding, deep-fry the squid just until golden and crisp, 1 1/2 to 2 minutes. Using a wire-mesh skimmer, transfer the squid to the wire racks and keep warm in the oven while deep-frying the rest. Don't hold the calamari in the oven for more than 5 minutes, or they may get soggy. Serve immediately, with the garlic mayonnaise for dipping.

NOTE: THIS RECIPE USES RAW EGG, WHICH HAS BEEN KNOWN TO CARRY SALMONELLA BACTERIA. YOU MAY USE 1/4 CUP LIQUID EGG SUBSTITUTE.

MAKES 4 TO 6 SERVINGS

Delmarva Crab Cakes with Cucumber Tartar Sauce

A perfect crab cake is plump and moist with a crisp crust and has enough spice to accent, not overpower, the crab.

1 To make the sauce: In a medium bowl, toss the cucumber with the salt. Let stand about 1 hour. Transfer to a sieve and rinse well under cold running water. Pat the cucumber dry.

2 In a small bowl, mix the drained cucumber, mayonnaise, scallion, capers, and anchovy paste. Cover and refrigerate for at least 1 hour. (The tartar sauce can be prepared up to 3 days ahead.)

3 To make the crab cakes: Mix the ½ cup bread crumbs, the mayonnaise, egg, mustard, scallion, Worcestershire sauce, and Delmarva seasoning. Mix in the crabmeat with wet hands, form into 6 cakes about 3 inches wide. Place the remaining ½ cup bread crumbs in a deep plate. Coat the crab cakes in the crumbs and set aside.

4 Line a baking sheet with paper towels. Into a large, deep skillet (preferably cast iron), pour vegetable oil to a depth of ½ inch, and heat over high heat until very hot but not smoking. Carefully add the crab cakes and cook, turning once, until golden brown, about 3 minutes. Using a slotted spatula, transfer to the paper towels to drain. Serve hot, with the tartar sauce on the side.

MAKES 6 CAKES

Delmarva Seasoning: Mix 2 teaspoons salt, l teaspoon cayenne pepper, l teaspoon ground celery seed, l teaspoon dry mustard, l teaspoon sweet paprika, l teaspoon ground black pepper, l teaspoon ground bay leaf, ¼ teaspoon ground cloves, ¼ teaspoon ground allspice, ¼ teaspoon ground ginger, ¼ teaspoon freshly grated nutmeg, ¼ teaspoon ground cardamom, and ¼ teaspoon ground cinnamon. Will keep indefinitely in a tightly covered container in a cool, dark place. Makes about 3 tablespoons.

Cucumber Tartar Sauce

1 cup ⅛-inch cubes peeled and seeded cucumber
½ teaspoon salt
½ cup mayonnaise
1 scallion, white and green parts, finely chopped
2 tablespoons nonpareil capers, rinsed
1 teaspoon anchovy paste

Crab Cakes

½ cup plus ⅓ cup dried bread crumbs
¼ cup mayonnaise
1 large egg, beaten
1 tablespoon Dijon mustard
1 scallion, white and green parts, finely chopped
½ teaspoon Worcestershire sauce
½ teaspoon Delmarva Seasoning (recipe below), or store-bought Old Bay Seasoning
1 pound fresh lump crabmeat, picked over for cartilage
Vegetable oil for deep-frying

the golden garden

vegetables & grains

Falafel on Greens

Falafel
½ cup fine bulgur wheat (see Note)

1½ cups cooked chickpeas
(garbanzo beans), or one 15-
ounce can chickpeas, drained
and rinsed

1 medium onion, chopped

¼ cup whole-wheat flour

1 large egg

2 tablespoons finely chopped fresh
parsley

2 garlic cloves, pressed

2 teaspoons ground cumin

1 teaspoon hot red pepper flakes

½ teaspoon salt

Tahini Dressing
½ cup water

½ cup tahini (sesame paste)

¼ cup fresh lemon juice

1 garlic clove, crushed through a
press

¼ teaspoon salt

¼ teaspoon hot red pepper sauce,
such as Tabasco

Vegetable shortening or oil for
deep-frying

8 ounces salad greens (about 8 cups)

2 ripe medium tomatoes, cut into
wedges

1 large cucumber, peeled and thinly
sliced

Cilantro sprigs for garnish

Falafel-stuffed pita sandwiches are familiar fare, but the bulgur and chickpea fritters are so tasty that I like to serve them with greens as a salad. While falafel are served all over the Middle East, it was Israeli immigrants that made them popular in this country.

1 To make the falafel: Put the bulgur in a medium bowl and add boiling water to cover by 2 inches. Let stand until the bulgur is tender, about 15 minutes. Drain well in a sieve, pressing lightly to remove excess liquid.

2 Line a baking sheet with waxed paper. In a food processor, pulse the chickpeas, onion, flour, egg, parsley, garlic, cumin, pepper flakes, and salt until they form a coarse puree. Add the bulgur, about ¼ cup at a time, pulsing after each addition, until the mixture is thick enough to form into balls. (You may not use all of the bulgur.) Using wet hands, form the mixture into 1-inch balls and place on the waxed paper. Cover loosely with plastic wrap and let stand for 1 hour.

3 Meanwhile, make the tahini dressing: In a blender, combine the water, tahini, lemon juice, garlic, salt, and pepper sauce. Process until smooth. Cover and refrigerate until ready to serve.

4 Preheat the oven to 200°F. Place a large wire cake rack over a jelly roll pan. In a deep Dutch oven, melt vegetable shortening over high heat to a depth of 2 to 3 inches and heat it to 365°F. In batches, without crowding, deep-fry the falafel until golden brown, about 3 minutes. Transfer to the wire rack and keep warm in the oven while frying the rest.

5 To serve, divide the greens, tomatoes, and cucumber among 6 large plates. Top each with six falafel and garnish with the cilantro sprigs. Serve immediately, with the dressing passed on the side.

NOTE: BULGUR IS DRIED, CRACKED WHEAT THAT REHYDRATES WHEN SOAKED IN LIQUID. IT CAN BE PROCESSED INTO FINE, MEDIUM, OR COARSE GRIND. USUALLY THE SUPERMARKET VARIETY IS THE FINE GRIND, WHICH IS PREFERABLE FOR MAKING FALAFEL.

MAKES 6 SERVINGS

Okra Fritters
with Chickpea Batter

There's no two ways about okra—you either love it or hate it. Deep-frying okra reduces its mucilaginous qualities, and when served to unsuspecting okra-haters, it can turn them into fans. Chickpea flour, also called garbanzo bean flour or *besan*, can be purchased at Indian markets and natural foods stores. Serve this as an appetizer at the beginning of an Asian meal.

1 Preheat the oven to 200°F. Line a baking sheet with waxed paper. Place a large wire cake rack over a jelly roll pan. In a deep Dutch oven, melt vegetable shortening to a depth of 2 to 3 inches and heat it to 365°F.

2 While the shortening is heating, beat the eggs in a shallow bowl. Put the chickpea flour, $\frac{1}{2}$ teaspoon salt, and pepper in another shallow bowl and stir to mix well. In batches, dip the okra in the egg, then in the chickpea flour. Deep-fry, without crowding, until golden brown, about 3 minutes. Using a wire-mesh skimmer, transfer the okra to the wire rack and keep warm in the oven while frying the rest. Season with salt and serve immediately, with the chutney for dipping.

MAKES 4 TO 6 SERVINGS

Vegetable shortening or oil for
  deep-frying
2 large eggs
$\frac{1}{2}$ cup chickpea flour (see recipe
  introduction)
$\frac{1}{2}$ teaspoon salt, plus more to taste
$\frac{1}{4}$ teaspoon freshly ground pepper
8 ounces fresh okra, stem end trimmed
Cilantro Chutney (page 44)

Vegetable Tempura

Ginger Dipping Sauce

⅓ cup shredded fresh ginger (use the
   large holes of a box grater)
½ cup Japanese soy sauce
¼ cup sweet sherry, such as oloroso
¼ cup rice vinegar
1 tablespoon packed light brown
   sugar

Vegetable Tempura

1½ pounds assorted vegetables, such
   as broccoli, cauliflower, small
   white mushrooms, red or green
   bell peppers, scallions, and sweet
   potatoes
1 cup white rice flour (available
   at natural foods stores) or
   all-purpose flour
¼ teaspoon baking powder
¾ cup ice water
1 large egg, beaten
Vegetable shortening or oil for
   deep-frying

For an authentic Japanese tempura batter, use rice flour. Because it has no gluten (which is the substance in wheat that gives a dough structure and strength), it makes a delicate batter. Be sure to use white rice flour, not brown, as the brown tends to scorch when deep-fried. If you are serving tempura as a main course, you'll want a variety of vegetables. Instead of buying them by the pound, head, or bunch, purchase precut vegetables from a salad bar.

1 To make the sauce: Place the ginger in a clean kitchen towel. Squeeze and wring the ginger over a bowl to extract the juice. Discard the pulp. You should have 2 tablespoons ginger juice.

2 In a small, nonreactive saucepan, bring the soy sauce, sherry, vinegar, and brown sugar to a boil over high heat and cook for 1 minute. Let cool completely. Stir in the ginger juice. (The sauce can be prepared up to 8 hours ahead, covered, and kept at room temperature.)

3 To make the tempura: Prepare the vegetables as follows:
Broccoli and cauliflower: Cut into 1-inch florets.
Red or green bell peppers: Discard seeds, ribs, and stems.
   Cut into ½-inch-wide by 2-inch-long strips.
Scallions: Cut off the green tops, leaving about 1 inch attached
   to the white portion. Save the green tops for another use.
Sweet potatoes: Peel and cut into ⅛-inch-thick rounds.

4 In a medium bowl, whisk the rice flour and baking powder to mix. Add the ice water and egg and stir just until combined (do not overmix).

5 Preheat the oven to 200°F. Place a large wire cake rack on a jelly roll pan. In a deep Dutch oven, melt vegetable shortening over high heat to a depth of 2 to 3 inches and heat it to 365°F. Working in batches, dip the vegetables in the batter, shaking off excess batter. Deep-fry until golden, 2 to 3 minutes. Transfer the vegetables to the wire rack to drain, and keep warm in the oven while frying the rest. If the batter thickens on standing, thin with a little water. Serve the tempura immediately, with the dipping sauce.

MAKES 4 TO 6 SERVINGS

Castroville Artichoke Sandwich

Virtually all of America's artichokes are grown in Castroville, California, just a short drive from where I grew up. In Castroville's restaurants, artichokes are served in just about every way imaginable. (I'm waiting for artichoke ice cream.) This is one of my favorites, and easy to make with frozen baby artichokes.

1 In a small bowl, mix the mayonnaise, lemon juice, and garlic. Set aside.

2 Line a baking sheet with waxed paper. Put the flour in a shallow bowl. In a medium bowl, beat the eggs with the oregano, salt, and pepper. One at a time, dip the artichoke hearts in the flour, then the eggs, then back into the flour. Place on the waxed paper.

3 Place a large wire cake rack over a jelly roll pan. In a deep Dutch oven, melt vegetable shortening over high heat to a depth of 2 to 3 inches and heat it to 365°F. Deep-fry the artichoke hearts until golden, about 3 minutes. Using a wire-mesh skimmer, transfer to the wire rack to drain briefly.

4 Split the rolls and pull some of the soft crumb from each roll to form a trench to hold the artichokes. Spread each roll with mayonnaise. Place equal amounts of the artichokes in each roll and serve immediately.

MAKES 3 SANDWICHES

¼ cup Garlic Mayonnaise (page 84) or store-bought mayonnaise
1 teaspoon fresh lemon juice
1 garlic clove, crushed through a press (if using store-bought mayonnaise)
1 cup all-purpose flour
2 large eggs
1 teaspoon dried oregano
½ teaspoon salt
¼ teaspoon freshly ground pepper
One 9-ounce package frozen artichoke hearts, thawed
Vegetable shortening or oil for deep-frying
Three 6-inch-long French or Italian sandwich rolls

Central Avenue Rice Balls with Mozzarella

1 tablespoon extra-virgin olive oil
1 cup finely chopped onion
1 1/2 cups Italian rice for risotto, such as Arborio
1 1/2 cups homemade or canned low-salt chicken broth
1 1/2 cups water
3/4 teaspoon salt
1/4 teaspoon freshly ground pepper
1 tablespoon tomato paste
1 tablespoon dry white wine, dry vermouth, or water
2/3 cup (3 ounces) freshly grated Parmigiano-Reggiano cheese
1/2 cup frozen peas, rinsed under hot water until thawed
2 large eggs
1 cup dried bread crumbs
2 ounces mozzarella cheese, preferably fresh, cut into fifteen 1/2-inch cubes
Vegetable shortening or oil for deep-frying

My neighborhood's main drag, Central Avenue, is lined with Italian delicatessens. Each shop vies for business, proclaiming to sell the best handmade mozzarella, nicknamed "mutz," and ricotta on the avenue (yes, they make their own on the premises). My favorite shop always sticks a rice ball into my order. They make a perfect lunch, served with a green salad and a glass of wine. If you'd like them for dinner, serve with Meaty Tomato Sauce (recipe on page 97).

1 In a medium saucepan, heat the oil over medium heat. Add the onion and cook, stirring occasionally, until softened, about 3 minutes. Add the rice and stir well. Add the broth, water, salt, and pepper. Bring to a boil, then reduce heat to low and cover. Simmer until the rice is tender and has absorbed the liquid, about 15 minutes.

2 In a medium bowl, dissolve the tomato paste in the wine. Add the rice, Parmigiano cheese, and peas and mix well. Let cool completely. (The mixture will thicken as it cools.)

3 Line a baking sheet with waxed paper. Beat the eggs in a medium bowl. Put the bread crumbs in a shallow bowl. With wet hands, place 1/3 cup of the rice mixture in one hand and flatten into a thick patty. Place a mozzarella cube in the center and cover it with the rice, forming it into a ball. Dip into the eggs, then roll in the bread crumbs to coat. Place on the waxed paper. Repeat to use the remaining rice, rinsing your hands often in water to keep the rice mixture from sticking. Refrigerate for 30 minutes to set the coating.

4 Position a rack in the center of the oven and preheat to 200°F. Place a large wire cake rack over a jelly roll pan. In a large Dutch oven, melt vegetable shortening over high heat to a depth of 3 inches and heat it to 350°F.

5 Fry 3 or 4 balls at a time, turning once, until golden brown, about 5 minutes. Using a wire-mesh skimmer, transfer to the cake rack and keep warm in the oven while frying the remaining balls. Serve the rice balls warm or at room temperature.

MAKES 15 RICE BALLS

Meaty Tomato Sauce: In a large saucepan, heat 2 tablespoons olive oil over medium heat. Add 1 medium onion, chopped, and cook until softened, about 3 minutes. Add 2 minced garlic cloves and cook for 1 minute. Add $1\frac{1}{2}$ pounds ground meat loaf combination (8 ounces each ground beef, ground pork, and ground veal). Cook, breaking up the meat into large chunks with a spoon, until seared, about 10 minutes. Add one 28-ounce can tomatoes in thick puree, chopped, one 8-ounce can tomato sauce, $\frac{1}{2}$ cup hearty red wine, 2 teaspoons dried oregano, 2 teaspoons dried basil, and $\frac{1}{4}$ teaspoon hot red pepper flakes. Bring to a boil over high heat, then reduce the heat to low. Simmer, stirring often, until the sauce thickens, about 2 hours. Skim off any fat on the surface. Serve hot. Makes about 4 cups.

VARIATION: REPLACE THE MOZZARELLA CUBES WITH ABOUT 2 TEASPOONS COOLED MEATY TOMATO SAUCE PER RICE BALL. SERVE THE FRIED BALLS WITH THE REMAINING SAUCE WARMED AND PASSED ON THE SIDE.

Roman Artichokes, ^{Jewish Style}

Deep-fried artichokes are a specialty in the restaurants of Rome's old Jewish sector. Looking like bronzed flowers, they are served with great flourish as an antipasto on folded linen napkins, though Americans may find them better suited as a side dish. The artichokes must be trimmed, which takes some practice, but once you master the technique, it's bound to become one of your favorite ways to eat artichokes. (This is one occasion when you should splurge on olive oil for frying.)

4 medium artichokes (7 ounces each),
    preferably with stems attached
2 lemons, halved
Olive oil for deep-frying
Salt to taste
Lemon wedges for serving

1 Working with 1 artichoke at a time, snap back the dark green tough outer leaves until you reach the inner cone of light green tender leaves. Cut off the top inch of the cone. As you work, rub the cut surfaces often with the lemon halves to prevent discoloring. Using a small sharp knife, pare the dark green skin from the bottom of the artichoke (and the stem, if attached). Place the artichoke upside down on a work surface and push down on it firmly so the leaves spread out—the artichoke will resemble a water lily. Using the tip of the knife, dig out the cluster of purple leaves in the center and scrape out the choke.

2 Place a large wire cake rack over a jelly roll pan. Pour 3 inches of oil into a Dutch oven. Over high heat, heat to 350°F. Deep-fry the artichokes until golden brown and tender, about 7 minutes. Using a wire-mesh skimmer, transfer the artichokes to the wire racks to drain briefly. Sprinkle with salt, then serve immediately, with the lemon wedges.

MAKES 6 SERVINGS

Broccoflower Fritti

Club Soda Batter

1 cup all-purpose flour
5 large eggs, beaten
2 tablespoons club soda
½ teaspoon salt
¼ teaspoon freshly ground pepper

Vegetable shortening or oil for
  deep-frying
1 head broccoflower (1¾ pounds),
  cut into bite-sized pieces
½ cup freshly grated Parmigiano-
  Reggiano cheese

Chartreuse-green broccoflower, looking like a science-fiction cross between broccoli and cauliflower, is showing up in more and more autumn markets. Deep-frying showcases its hearty flavor. This excellent all-purpose batter, lightened with a splash of club soda, could also be used with other vegetables, including broccoli or cauliflower florets, of course.

1 To make the batter: In a medium bowl, stir the flour, eggs, club soda, salt, and pepper together just until combined. Do not overmix.

2 Preheat the oven to 200°F. Place a large wire cake rack over a jelly roll pan. In a deep Dutch oven, melt vegetable shortening over high heat to a depth of 2 to 3 inches and heat it to 365°F. In batches, without crowding, dip the broccoflower pieces in the batter and deep-fry until golden brown, about 2 minutes. Using a wire-mesh strainer, transfer to the wire rack and keep warm in the oven while frying the rest. Place the broccoflower on a serving platter, sprinkle with the cheese, and serve immediately.

MAKES 8 SERVINGS

Chinese Green Beans

The classic version of this recipe uses long beans, which have a slightly shriveled appearance and a mild asparagus flavor. They can be found in Asian markets, but common green beans also like to be cooked this way. Deep-frying green or long beans does not crisp them, but it does intensify their flavor. This is a good way to add interest to what can sometimes be a mundane vegetable.

1 Heat a large, flat-bottomed wok or large Dutch oven over high heat. Add enough oil to come one-third the way up the sides of the wok or 3 inches deep in the Dutch oven. Heat over high heat until very hot, but not smoking (the surface of the oil will shimmer slightly), or a deep-frying thermometer reads 365°F. While the oil is heating, mix the soy sauce, sherry, rice vinegar, sesame oil, sugar, and salt in a small bowl and set aside.

2 Line a baking sheet with paper towels. In batches, without crowding, deep-fry the beans until crisp-tender and slightly shriveled, about 1 minute. Using a wire-mesh skimmer, transfer the beans to the paper towels and drain.

3 Pour off all but 1 tablespoon of the oil and return the pan to high heat. Add the ginger, garlic, and chilies and stir-fry until fragrant, about 15 seconds. Stir the soy sauce mixture well and stir it into the pan. Return the beans to the pan and stir-fry until coated with the sauce. Serve immediately.

MAKES 6 SERVINGS

Vegetable oil for deep-frying
2 tablespoons Japanese soy sauce
2 tablespoons dry sherry
1 tablespoon rice vinegar
1 tablespoon Asian dark sesame oil
1 teaspoon sugar
¼ teaspoon salt
12 ounces green or long beans, trimmed and cut into 3- to 4-inch lengths
2 teaspoons shredded fresh ginger
3 garlic cloves, minced
4 small whole dried red chilies

Vidalia Onion Rings
with Ale Batter

One of life's big unanswerable questions is: What is better with hamburgers, onion rings or French fries? These onion rings are world class. Ale makes a light, fluffy, crisp coating and gives the batter more flavor than the traditional lager beer. Regular Spanish yellow onions can be used in place of sweet onions. Like most deep-fried treats, these should be served as soon as possible after cooking.

1 Use only the large outer rings of the onions, saving the smaller rings (less than 1 inch in diameter) for another use. Soak the onion rings in a large bowl of ice water for 30 minutes. Drain well (give them a whirl in a salad spinner, if you like) and pat dry with paper towels.

2 Meanwhile, to make the batter: In a medium bowl, whisk the flour, cornstarch, Bayou Seasoning, and salt together. Add the egg and oil. Using a wooden spoon (not a whisk), stir in enough ale to make a thick, clinging batter—do not overmix. Let stand at room temperature for 30 minutes.

3 Preheat the oven to 200°F. Place a large wire cake rack over a jelly roll pan. In a deep Dutch oven over high heat, melt vegetable shortening to a depth of 2 to 3 inches and heat it to 365°F. In batches, without crowding, dip the onion rings in the batter, letting excess batter drip back into the bowl, then place in the hot oil. Deep-fry until golden brown, 2 to 3 minutes. Using a wire-mesh skimmer, transfer the rings to the wire rack and keep warm in the oven while frying the rest. Season with salt, and serve immediately.

Makes 4 to 6 servings

2 large sweet onions, such as Vidalia, Maui, or Walla Walla, cut into 1/2-inch-thick rings

Ale Batter
3/4 cup all-purpose flour
1/4 cup cornstarch
2 teaspoons Bayou Seasoning (page 78)
1 teaspoon salt
1 large egg, beaten
2 tablespoons vegetable oil
3/4 cup ale, as needed

Vegetable shortening or oil for deep-frying
Salt to taste

Potato-Pesto Puffs

1 pound red-skinned potatoes, peeled
  and cut into 2-inch chunks
⅓ cup freshly grated Parmigiano-
  Reggiano cheese
2 tablespoons chopped fresh basil
2 large eggs, separated
2 garlic cloves, crushed through a
  press
¼ teaspoon salt
¼ teaspoon freshly ground pepper
½ cup dried bread crumbs
Vegetable shortening or oil for
  deep-frying

I learned to make these years ago from an Italian cook who whipped them up from cold mashed potatoes. I rarely have a surfeit of left-over mashed potatoes, so now I start from scratch when I make these cheesey puffs. They are an excellent side dish for grilled fish fillets.

1 Add the potatoes to a large pot of lightly salted water and bring to a boil over high heat. Reduce heat to medium and cook until tender, 20 to 25 minutes. Drain well. Transfer to a medium bowl.

2 Using a hand-held electric mixer or a potato masher, mash the potatoes. Let cool slightly. Beat in the cheese, basil, egg yolks, garlic, salt, and pepper. Let cool until tepid.

3 Line a baking sheet with waxed paper. Put the egg whites in a medium bowl and beat until foamy. Place the bread crumbs in a shallow bowl. Form the potato mixture into balls, about 1 tablespoon each. One at a time, coat each ball with the egg white, then roll in the bread crumbs. Place on the waxed paper.

4 Place a large wire cake rack over a jelly roll pan. In a deep Dutch oven over high heat, melt vegetable shortening to a depth of 2 to 3 inches and heat it to 365°F. In batches, deep-fry the potato balls until golden brown, about 3 minutes. Using a wire-mesh skimmer, transfer to the wire rack and keep warm in the oven while frying the rest. Serve immediately.

MAKES ABOUT 18 PUFFS

Panisses
(Chickpea Fries)

To Americans who love fine restaurants, the word *Panisse* means **Chez Panisse, Alice Waters's seminal restaurant in Berkeley. To French movie lovers, it refers to a character (after whom the restaurant is named) in the beloved Marcel Pagnol film trilogy of** *Fanny, César,* **and** *Marius,* **who, in turn, was named for these Provençal chickpea-flour "fries." Cooks familiar with polenta will recognize the procedure: The flour is cooked into a thick mush, cooled, then cut into sticks before frying. Serve panisses with grilled marinated lamb steak to make a variation of the bistro classic "steak frites."**

1½ cups homemade or low-salt
    canned chicken broth
1½ cups water
1 teaspoon salt
½ teaspoon freshly ground pepper
1½ cups chickpea flour
Olive oil for deep-frying

1 Thoroughly oil an 8-by-11-inch baking dish. In a medium, heavy saucepan, combine the broth, water, salt, and pepper. Bring to a boil over high heat. Whisking constantly, gradually add the chickpea flour. Reduce heat to medium-low. Simmer the chickpea mixture, whisking constantly, until thick and smooth (it will seem that the lumps will never disappear), about 5 minutes. Scrape into the prepared pan and spread evenly with an oiled spatula or pat smooth with oiled hands. Let cool completely.

2 Hold a baking sheet over the dish and invert to unmold the cooled chickpea mixture onto the sheet. Using an oiled sharp knife, cut lengthwise into thirds, then crosswise into eighths to make 24 "steak fry"–shaped panisses.

3 Preheat the oven to 200°F. Place a wire cake rack over a jelly roll pan. Into a deep Dutch oven, pour oil to a depth of 2 to 3 inches. Heat it to 365°F over high heat. In batches, without crowding, deep-fry the panisses until golden brown, about 3 minutes. Using a wire-mesh skimmer, transfer the panisses to the wire rack and keep warm in the oven while frying the rest. Serve immediately.

MAKES ABOUT 24 "FRIES"

Classic Belgian French Fries

In Belgium, deep-fried potatoes are the national dish, and Brussels seems to have a *frietje* stand on every corner. Just don't try telling a Belgian that their beloved fries are French. Many historians believe what French cooks call *pommes frites* were originated by Belgian peasants as far back as the seventeenth century. Of course, being so close to each other, the two countries share many recipes (and words, as *frites* and *frietjes* are surely related). When the American soldiers returned home after World War I, they brought back with them memories of the fried potato sticks they had in France, and called them "French" fries.

You could serve these Belgian style, with mayonnaise standing in for ketchup, or with my favorite dip: mayonnaise and ketchup mixed in equal amounts. For the best fries, use mature baking potatoes and a two-step frying process. The fries must be at room temperature before their second immersion, so be sure to allow enough time between the steps. There is a whole school of fried potato dishes in French cuisine, and recipes for some of them follow the classic instructions for French fries—but note that the gaufrettes and shoestring potatoes in the recipes below get only one trip to the deep fryer.

3 large baking potatoes, such as russet or Idaho (2 pounds)
Vegetable shortening or oil for deep-frying
Salt to taste
Mayonnaise (page 84, made without garlic), ketchup, or a combination, for dipping

1 Starting at least 30 minutes or up to 4 hours before serving, scrub the potatoes well under cold running water. Peel them, if desired. Using a sharp knife or a French fry cutter, cut each potato lengthwise into long sticks about ¼ inch square. Place in a large bowl of cold water. (If you like crispy fries, refrigerate the bowl of fries for 2 hours.) Drain well. In batches, spin the potatoes in a salad spinner, then pat completely dry with paper towels. Wrap the potatoes in paper towels to keep them from discoloring.

2 Place a large wire cake rack over a jelly roll pan. In a deep Dutch oven over high heat, melt shortening to a depth of 2 to 3 inches and heat it to 325°F. In batches, without crowding, deep-fry the potatoes until tender and just beginning to color, about 3 minutes. Using a wire-mesh skimmer, transfer to the wire rack and let cool. The potatoes can stand at room temperature for up to 4 hours.

continued ➔

3 Preheat the oven to 200°F. Transfer the cooled potatoes to paper towels and pat to remove excess fat. Reheat the shortening over high heat to 375°F. In batches, without crowding, add the potatoes and cook until crisp and golden brown, 1 to 2 minutes. Using a wire-mesh skimmer, transfer the fries to the wire rack and keep warm in the oven while frying the rest. Serve immediately, seasoned with salt and with a dipping sauce on the side.

MAKES 4 SERVINGS

GAUFRETTES (WAFFLE-CUT POTATOES): Cut the ends off a potato to make it somewhat rectangular. Using the ruffled blade of a mandoline, cut the potato end to make a ridged surface. Turn the potato 90 degrees and slice again to make a waffle-cut chip. Continue cutting and turning the potato until all of it has been sliced. Repeat with the remaining potatoes. Transfer to a bowl of cold water and let stand for 5 minutes. Drain, spin in a salad spinner, and pat dry with paper towels. Deep-fry in 375°F vegetable oil until crisp and golden, about 3 minutes.

SHOESTRING POTATOES: Using a mandoline, cut the potatoes lengthwise into 1/16-inch square "shoestrings." Transfer to a bowl of cold water and proceed as for the gaufrettes above.

It's a fact that the most delicious French fries are cooked in rendered lard or beef fat. (McDonald's fries haven't been quite the same since they stopped using beef fat.)

Potato Pancakes (Latkes)

The tradition of serving potato pancakes (latkes) at Hanukkah is related to their being fried in oil, and has nothing to do with potatoes themselves. The holiday celebrates the miraculous burning of a temple lamp that was supposedly empty of oil, so fried foods are in order. To make sure the pancakes don't fall apart, the potato starch from the squeezed shredded potatoes is stirred back into the latke mixture. One of my favorite ways to serve latkes is for brunch, topped with smoked salmon, sour cream, and chives.

3 large baking potatoes, such as russet or Idaho (2 pounds)
1 large egg, beaten
1 teaspoon salt
$\frac{1}{4}$ teaspoon freshly ground pepper
Vegetable oil for frying
Sour cream for serving

1 Peel the potatoes. Shred them on the large holes of a box grater or in a food processor, and put the shredded potatoes in a medium bowl. A handful at a time, squeeze the liquid from the potatoes back into the bowl and place the squeezed potatoes in a second bowl. Carefully pour off and discard the cloudy liquid from the first bowl, leaving the white potato starch that has sunk to the bottom. Scrape the potato starch into the shredded potatoes. Add the egg, salt, and pepper and mix well.

2 Preheat the oven to 200°F. Place a large wire cake rack over a jelly roll pan. In a large, deep skillet over medium-high heat, heat $\frac{1}{2}$ inch of vegetable oil until very hot, but not smoking. In batches, carefully add about $\frac{1}{3}$ cup batter for each latke to the oil and form into 4-inch-diameter pancakes. Fry, turning once, until golden brown on both sides, about 6 minutes. Transfer to the wire rack and keep warm while frying the remaining latkes. Don't worry if the remaining potato mixture turns brown while standing. Pour off any liquid from the potato mixture before making the remaining latkes. Serve immediately, with the sour cream.

MAKES ABOUT 8 LATKES

Zucchini and Ricotta Fritters

1 medium zucchini, shredded on the
    large holes of a box grater
½ teaspoon plus ⅛ teaspoon salt
8 ounces ricotta cheese (1 cup)
¼ cup freshly grated Parmigiano-
    Reggiano cheese
¼ cup all-purpose flour
1 large egg
1 large egg yolk
1 tablespoon chopped fresh basil
1 garlic clove, crushed through a
    press
⅛ teaspoon freshly ground pepper
Vegetable shortening or oil for
    deep-frying

Zucchini takes well to deep-frying, with fried zucchini sticks being a favorite dish. These fritters are much more elegant, and are equally at home as an appetizer or as a side dish for roast chicken.

1 Put the zucchini in a medium bowl and toss with ½ teaspoon salt. Let stand until the zucchini releases its juices, about 30 minutes. Drain in a wire sieve and rinse well under cold running water. Drain again. One handful at a time, squeeze the excess liquid from the zucchini and transfer the zucchini to another medium bowl.

2 Add the ricotta cheese, Parmigiano cheese, flour, egg, egg yolk, basil, garlic, the remaining ⅛ teaspoon salt, and the pepper and mix well.

3 Preheat the oven to 200°F. Place a large wire cake rack over a jelly roll pan. In a deep Dutch oven, melt vegetable shortening over high heat to a depth of 2 to 3 inches and heat it to 365°F. In batches, without crowding, carefully drop tablespoonfuls of the zucchini-ricotta mixture into the hot oil. Deep-fry until golden, about 3 minutes. Using a wire-mesh skimmer, transfer the fritters to the wire rack and keep warm in the oven while frying the rest. Serve immediately.

MAKES 12 FRITTERS

Zucchini Blossoms

Zucchini blossoms can be picked from your own plants or purchased at farmer's markets in late summer. If you buy them at the right time in the season, they can be downright cheap—I recently paid $1.50 for a bag of 60 blossoms! (Because they won't mature into zucchini, some gardening cooks only pick the male blossoms—males are straight at the blossom end, where the females are bulbous. But my bag contained female blossoms, too, because, as the farmer explained, it's a way of controlling how much zucchini will need to be harvested.) Dipped in a white wine–based batter, they make one of the most delicious, yet most delicate, of all fritters. It is important to use a full-flavored wine for the tastiest batter.

1 Pull out the large pistil from the center of each blossom. (If the zucchini blossoms are closed, make a slit in the side to reach the pistil.) Cut off all but 1 inch of the stem. Wipe the blossoms carefully with a damp kitchen towel. Set aside.

2 To make the Chardonnay batter: About 1 hour before deep-frying, mix the flour, 1 cup of the wine, the egg yolk, basil, garlic, salt, and pepper in a medium bowl just until combined. The batter will be slightly lumpy. Let stand for at least 30 minutes or up to 1 hour.

3 Stir the remaining $\frac{1}{4}$ cup wine into the batter. In a medium bowl, beat the egg white until soft peaks form, and fold the beaten white into the batter.

4 Preheat the oven to 200°F. Place a large wire cake rack over a jelly roll pan. Pour 2 to 3 inches oil into a deep Dutch oven. Heat over high heat to 365°F. Working in batches, hold the zucchini flowers by the stems and dip them one at a time into the batter, letting the excess batter drip back into the bowl. In batches, without crowding, deep-fry the blossoms until golden, turning once, about 2 minutes. Using a wire-mesh skimmer, transfer to the wire rack and keep warm in the oven while frying the rest. Serve immediately.

MAKES 18 FRITTERS

18 zucchini blossoms, preferably with stems attached

Chardonnay Batter
1 cup all-purpose flour
1$\frac{1}{4}$ cups full-bodied dry white wine, such as Chardonnay
1 large egg, separated
1 tablespoon finely chopped fresh basil
1 garlic clove, crushed through a press
$\frac{1}{2}$ teaspoon salt
$\frac{1}{4}$ teaspoon freshly ground pepper

Vegetable oil for deep-frying

fried & true

***to a* crisp**

desserts & sweet pastries

Cannoli

Orange-Ricotta Filling

4 cups (2 pounds) whole-milk ricotta
    cheese
¼ cup confectioners' sugar
3 tablespoons orange-flavored
    liqueur, such as Grand Marnier
Grated zest of 1 orange

Cannoli Dough

2 cups all-purpose flour
1½ tablespoons granulated sugar
¼ teaspoon ground cinnamon
⅛ teaspoon salt
¼ cup chilled vegetable shortening,
    plus more for deep-frying
⅓ cup sweet Marsala or water
2 tablespoons red wine vinegar
1 large egg
1 large egg white, beaten until foamy,
    for sealing dough

2 ounces high-quality bittersweet
    chocolate
Confectioners' sugar for dusting

Cannoli start as rounds of pastry wrapped around metal tubes. When deep-fried, the pastry turns into crisp sleeves that are then stuffed with ricotta or pastry cream. This recipe is based on one from my friend Angela Emmi, who made cannoli by the dozens for her catering business. While Angela's recipe calls for water, I like to use sweet Marsala wine instead. Cannoli tubes, available at kitchenware shops, come in different lengths, so the size and yield of your cannoli depends on the size of your molds. You will need at least four 4-inch-long molds for this recipe.

1 To make the filling: Rub the ricotta through a coarse-meshed sieve into a medium bowl. Stir in the confectioners' sugar, liqueur, and orange zest. Cover and refrigerate until ready to use.

2 To make the dough: In a food processor, pulse the flour, sugar, cinnamon, and salt to mix. Add the ¼ cup shortening and pulse until the mixture resembles coarse meal with a few pea-sized bits. In a glass measuring cup, mix the Marsala, vinegar, and egg. With the machine running, add the liquid through the feed tube and process until a ball forms on top of the blade. Process for 20 seconds to knead the dough. To make the dough by hand, stir the flour, sugar, cinnamon, and salt together in a large bowl. Add the shortening and cut it in with a pastry blender or 2 knives until the mixture resembles coarse crumbs. Stir in the wine mixture to form a soft dough. Transfer to a lightly floured work surface and knead just until the dough is smooth and supple, about 5 minutes. Wrap the ball of dough with plastic wrap. Let stand at room temperature for 30 minutes.

3 Place a large wire cake rack over a jelly roll pan. In a deep Dutch oven, melt vegetable shortening over high heat to a depth of 2 to 3 inches and heat it to 365°F.

4 Working with one half of the dough at a time, roll it out on a lightly floured surface until ¹⁄₁₆ inch thick. Using a saucer as a guide, cut out rounds that are slightly less wide than the length of the cannoli tubes (for example, just less than 4 inches wide for 4-inch-long tubes). Wrap a pastry round around each tube, overlapping the ends and securing the round closed with a dab of egg white. Do not get any egg white on the tube, or it will glue the pastry to the tube.

5 Deep-fry 2 tubes (it is hard to keep track of more than 2 at a time) until golden brown, about 1 minute. Using kitchen tongs, carefully transfer the tubes to the wire rack to drain. Let cool for about 2 minutes and, holding the tube with the kitchen tongs (the tube will be hot), slide the cannoli shell from the tube. Let the tubes cool (no need to wash them) while frying the other 2 tubes. Continue forming and frying the cannoli shells until all the dough is used. Let the fried shells cool completely. Do not reroll any scraps. If you wish, cut them into cookie-sized portions, deep-fry until golden, dust with confectioners' sugar, and serve as cookies.

6 To keep the cannoli shells from softening, fill them no more than 1 hour before serving. Put the filling in a pastry bag fitted with a No. 5 plain tip (a ½-inch-wide opening). Pipe the filling into the pastry shells, filling first one side of the shell, and then the other. To garnish, grate chocolate over the exposed filling and sift confectioners' sugar over the cannoli.

MAKES ABOUT TWENTY 4-INCH CANNOLI

Chocolate-Orange Churros

½ cup water

½ cup (1 stick) unsalted butter, cut into ½-inch pieces

2 tablespoons granulated sugar

Grated zest of 1 orange

½ teaspoon salt

1 cup all-purpose flour

4 large eggs, beaten

1 teaspoon vanilla extract

Vegetable shortening or oil for deep-frying

½ cup confectioners' sugar

3 tablespoons unsweetened cocoa powder

¼ teaspoon ground cinnamon

When I was at the University of Guadalajara, my breakfast, like that of millions of Mexicans, was hot chocolate and churros, deep-fried ridged crullers sprinkled with confectioners' sugar. My version uses the traditional cream puff–like dough, but it is perked up with orange zest and coated with cocoa powder. You'll need a large pastry bag fitted with a fluted tip to shape the churros.

1 In a medium, heavy saucepan, combine the water, butter, granulated sugar, orange zest, and salt. Boil over medium heat, stirring occasionally so that the butter is completely melted by the time the water boils. Add the flour and stir until the dough forms a ball that leaves the sides of the pan and begins to film the bottom of the pan, about 1½ minutes. Remove from heat and let cool for 2 minutes. Gradually beat in the eggs, then the vanilla. Transfer to a pastry bag fitted with a No. 5 fluted tip (a ½-inch-wide opening).

2 Preheat the oven to 200°F. Place a large wire cake rack over a jelly roll pan. In a deep Dutch oven, melt vegetable shortening over high heat to a depth of 2 to 3 inches and heat to 375°F. In batches, without crowding, pipe 4- to 5-inch lengths of dough into the hot shortening, cutting off each length with a small sharp knife. Deep-fry until golden brown, about 2½ minutes. Using a wire-mesh skimmer, transfer the churros to the wire rack to drain, and keep warm in the oven while frying the rest.

3 In a small bowl, mix the confectioners' sugar, cocoa, and cinnamon and place in a wire sieve. Sift the mixture over the churros and serve immediately.

MAKES 20 CHURROS

Fried Custard Squares

When chilled custard squares are coated in bread crumbs and deep-fried, they become crunchy on the outside and creamy within. Cool berries are the perfect counterpoint to the warm custards.

1 Lightly butter an 8-by-11-inch glass baking dish. In a medium saucepan, bring the milk, lemon zest, and cinnamon stick to a simmer over low heat. Let stand for 5 minutes. Remove and discard the lemon zest and cinnamon.

2 In a medium bowl, whisk the egg yolks, sugar, and cornstarch together. Gradually whisk in the hot milk. Rinse out the saucepan and return the custard to the pan. Stirring constantly with a wooden spatula, bring to a boil over medium heat. Stir in the vanilla. Strain through a fine-meshed sieve into the prepared dish and smooth the top.

3 Place piece of buttered waxed paper directly on top of the custard, buttered-side down, and pierce the paper a few times to allow the steam to escape. Place on a wire cake rack and let cool until tepid. Refrigerate until firm and chilled, at least 4 hours or overnight.

4 Remove the waxed paper. Hold a baking sheet over the dish and invert them together to unmold the custard onto the sheet. Cut the custard into 12 equal rectangles.

5 Line a baking sheet with waxed paper. In a shallow bowl, beat the eggs well. Place the bread crumbs in another shallow bowl. Coat each custard rectangle evenly with the eggs, then the bread crumbs, patting to help the crumbs adhere. Place on the waxed paper.

6 Preheat the oven to 200°F. Line a baking sheet with paper towels. In a deep Dutch oven, melt vegetable shortening over high heat to a depth of 2 to 3 inches and heat it to 365°F. In batches, without crowding, deep-fry the custards until golden brown, about 3 minutes. Using a slotted spatula, transfer the custards to the paper towels to drain, and keep warm in the oven while frying the rest. Serve immediately, garnished with the berries.

MAKES 6 SERVINGS

2 cups milk
Zest of 1 lemon, removed in strips
    with a vegetable peeler
1 cinnamon stick
6 large egg yolks
$\frac{1}{2}$ cup sugar
$\frac{1}{3}$ cup cornstarch
1 teaspoon vanilla extract
2 large eggs
2 cups fresh Italian bread crumbs,
    preferably from day-old bread
Vegetable shortening or oil for
    deep-frying
3 cups assorted fresh berries, such
    as raspberries, blueberries, and
    sliced strawberries

Orchard Buttermilk Doughnuts

When I was testing the recipes for this book, I put these dough-nuts out on a plate in my building's foyer so my neighbors could grab them on their way to work (and keep me from eating the whole batch!). Later in the morning, I got phone calls from people saying that these warm, spicy doughnuts had made their day. It's true: They are everything that a doughnut should be.

1 In a medium bowl, combine 1½ cups of the flour, the sugar, baking powder, baking soda, cinnamon, nutmeg, and salt. Add the 2 tablespoons shortening. Using a hand-held electric mixer at medium speed, mix until the shortening is cut into very fine crumbs, about 2 minutes.

2 In a medium bowl, combine the buttermilk, eggs, and vanilla. Beat until smooth and stir into the flour mixture. Gradually stir in the remaining 1¾ cups flour to make a soft dough. On a lightly floured surface, gently knead the dough just until smooth, about 1 minute.

3 Line a baking sheet with waxed paper. Place a large wire cake rack over a jelly roll pan. In a deep Dutch oven, melt vegetable shortening over high heat to a depth of 2 to 3 inches and heat it to 375°F.

4 On a lightly floured work surface, pat the dough out into a thick rectangle and dust the top with flour. Roll out the dough until ½ inch thick. Using a doughnut cutter, cut out the doughnuts. Or, use a 3-inch round biscuit cutter to cut out the doughnuts and a 1¼-inch round cutter to cut out the holes. Cut straight down, without twisting the cutter, so the doughnuts will rise properly when deep-fried. Transfer the doughnuts and holes to the waxed paper. Gather up the dough, knead gently, and reroll until all of the doughnuts have been cut out.

continued ➡

3¼ cups all-purpose flour

1 cup sugar

2 teaspoons baking powder

1 teaspoon baking soda

½ teaspoon ground cinnamon

½ teaspoon freshly grated nutmeg

½ teaspoon salt

2 tablespoons chilled vegetable shortening, plus more for deep frying

¾ cup buttermilk

2 large eggs, beaten

1 teaspoon vanilla extract

Apple Cider Glaze

1½ cups confectioners' sugar

¼ cup apple juice, heated to boiling

5 In batches, slip a metal spatula under one doughnut at a time and lower it into the hot shortening. Deep-fry without crowding, turning once, until golden brown, 3 to 4 minutes. Using a wire-mesh skimmer, transfer to the wire racks to drain. When all of the doughnuts have been fried, fry the doughnut holes until golden brown, about 2 minutes. Let them cool completely.

6 To make the glaze: In a small bowl, whisk the confectioners' sugar and boiling cider together. Holding them by the edges, briefly dip the doughnuts into the glaze, letting the excess drip back into the bowl. Place the doughnuts, iced sides up, on a wire cake rack to set the icing. The doughnuts are best served the day they are made.

MAKES TWELVE 3-INCH DOUGHNUTS

Fattigmans Bakkels

(Fried Diamond Cookies)

Every European country has a special fried Christmas cookie. This one was originally very simple, made from a plain dough with only a dusting of confectioners' sugar for embellishment. In fact, the name means "poor man's cookies" in Norwegian. Over the years, cooks have added more upscale ingredients, like heavy cream, cardamom, and brandy, to make these quite rich (and delicious).

1 In a large bowl, combine the eggs, egg yolk, sugar, cream, brandy, cardamom, and salt. Beat until smooth. Using a wooden spoon, stir in the flour to make a stiff dough. Form into a ball, wrap in plastic wrap, and let stand for 15 minutes.

2 Line a baking sheet with waxed paper. Divide the dough in half. Keeping one half covered, put the other half of the dough on a well-floured work surface and flatten into a thick disk. Dust the top of the dough with flour and roll out $1/16$ inch thick. Using a fluted pastry wheel or a sharp knife, cut the dough into diamond shapes 4 inches long and 1 inch wide. Set aside on the waxed paper.

3 Line a jelly roll pan with crumpled paper towels. In a deep Dutch oven, melt vegetable shortening over high heat to a depth of 2 to 3 inches and heat it to 375°F. In batches, without crowding, deep-fry the cookies, turning once, until golden, about $1/2$ minutes. Using a wire-mesh skimmer, transfer to the paper towels to drain. Separate each new layer of cookies with more paper towels. Let the cookies cool completely. Sift the confectioners' sugar over the cookies. Store the cookies in an airtight container in a cool place for up to 1 week.

MAKES ABOUT $7^{1}/_{2}$ DOZEN COOKIES

2 large eggs
1 large egg yolk
3 tablespoons granulated sugar
3 tablespoons heavy cream
1 tablespoon brandy or dark rum
$1/8$ teaspoon ground cardamom
$1/8$ teaspoon salt
About $1^{1}/_{2}$ cups all-purpose flour
Vegetable shortening or oil for deep-frying
Confectioners' sugar for dusting

Malasadas

(Portuguese Doughnuts)

½ cup milk
4 tablespoons (½ stick) unsalted
    butter
2 tablespoons sugar
1½ teaspoons active dry yeast
¼ cup warm (105° to 115°F) water
3 cups all-purpose flour
½ teaspoon salt
2 large eggs, beaten
Vegetable shortening or oil for
    deep-frying
½ cup sugar
¼ teaspoon ground cinnamon

These cinnamon sugar–coated yeast doughnuts are popular in Portuguese-American communities from Newark, New Jersey (near where I live now), to Oakland, California (my hometown). I remember these as a staple at church fund-raisers, made by a battalion of Portuguese women.

1 In a small saucepan, heat the milk, butter, and sugar over low heat until the butter melts. Remove from heat and let stand until tepid.

2 In a small bowl, sprinkle the yeast over the warm water and let stand until creamy, about 5 minutes. Stir until dissolved.

3 Lightly butter a medium bowl. In a food processor, pulse the flour and salt to combine. With the machine running, add the yeast mixture, then the milk mixture and eggs. Process until the mixture forms a soft dough. To make the dough by hand, mix the flour and salt in a large bowl. Stir in the yeast mixture, milk mixture, and eggs to make a soft dough.

4 Transfer to a lightly floured work surface and knead just until smooth, 3 to 5 minutes. Do not overknead the dough. Transfer the dough to the bowl and turn to coat the dough with butter. Cover the bowl tightly with plastic wrap. Let stand in a warm place until almost doubled (if you insert a finger ½ inch into the dough, it will leave an impression), about 1½ hours.

5 Punch down the dough, turn it again to coat lightly with butter, and cover. Let rise again until almost doubled, about 45 minutes.

6 Line a large baking sheet with waxed paper. Divide the dough into 16 pieces and roll each into a ball. Place a ball on an unfloured work surface. Roll the dough underneath your hands, moving your hands apart in a horizontal movement while rolling, until the dough is rolled and stretched into a 6-inch rope about ½ inch wide. Place on the waxed paper and cover loosely with plastic wrap. Repeat with the remaining dough.

7 Place a large wire cake rack over a jelly roll pan. In a deep Dutch oven, melt vegetable shortening over high heat to a depth of 2 to 3 inches and heat it to 365°F. In batches, without crowding, deep-fry the doughnuts, turning once, until golden brown, about 3 minutes. Using a wire-mesh skimmer, transfer to the wire rack to drain.

8 In a large paper bag, mix the sugar and cinnamon. Add a few doughnuts at a time to the bag, close the bag, and shake it to coat the doughnuts. Serve warm or at room temperature.

MAKES 16 MALASADAS

Mango Chimichangas
with Raspberry Sauce

Raspberry Sauce
12 ounces fresh or frozen
    raspberries (3 cups)
1/4 cup granulated sugar
1 tablespoon fresh lime juice

Mango Chimichangas
4 ripe medium mangoes
1/3 cup granulated sugar
1 tablespoon fresh lime juice
1 teaspoon cornstarch
Grated zest of 1 lime
Four 10-inch flour tortillas
Vegetable shortening or oil for
    deep-frying
Confectioners' sugar for dusting

These sweet deep-fried burritos are stuffed with mangoes and tossed with lime juice. Make these in the late spring when mangoes are at the peak of their season and reasonably priced.

1 To make the sauce: In a blender or food processor, puree the raspberries, sugar, and lime juice. Strain through a fine-meshed sieve into a small bowl to remove the raspberry seeds. Cover and refrigerate until ready to serve.

2 To make the chimichangas: Lay a mango on a work surface, plump side down. The mango pit is long and flat, and runs horizontally through the fruit, so the trick is to cut the flesh away without hitting the pit. Using a sharp, thin-bladed knife, slice off the top third of the mango, cutting around the pit. Turn the mango over and slice off the other side. Repeat with the remaining mangoes. One piece at a time, using a large serving spoon, scoop out the mango flesh in one piece from the peel. Cut the mango flesh into 3/4-inch cubes. Place in a medium bowl and toss with the granulated sugar, lime juice, cornstarch, and lime zest.

3 In a dry medium skillet over medium heat, heat a tortilla, turning once, until pliable, about 30 seconds. Place on a work surface. Place one fourth of the mango mixture on the bottom third of the tortilla, leaving a 1-inch border. Fold up the bottom of the tortilla to enclose the filling, fold in the sides, and roll up into a thick cylinder. Secure the chimichanga closed with wooden toothpicks. Repeat with the remaining tortillas and filling.

4 Preheat the oven to 200°F. Place a large wire cake rack over a jelly roll pan. In a deep Dutch oven, melt vegetable shortening over high heat to a depth of 2 to 3 inches and heat it to 365°F. In batches, without crowding, deep-fry the chimichangas until golden, about 3 minutes. Using kitchen tongs, transfer the chimichangas to the wire rack to drain, and keep warm in the oven while frying the rest.

5 To serve, spoon equal amounts of the sauce into the centers of 4 dinner plates. Place a chimichanga on each plate and sift confectioners' sugar over the entire plate. Serve immediately.

MAKES 4 CHIMICHANGAS

Pennsylvania Funnel Cakes

Vegetable shortening or oil for
  deep-frying
1 1/2 cups milk
2 large eggs
2 2/3 cups all-purpose flour
1/4 cup granulated sugar
2 teaspoons baking soda
1 1/2 teaspoons baking powder
1/2 teaspoon salt
Confectioners' sugar for dusting, or
  melted butter and warmed maple
  syrup for serving

Funnel cakes are sold throughout Pennsylvania Dutch country, usu-ally as a sugar-coated hand-held snack. They were orginally shaped by passing the thick batter through the opening of a funnel into hot shortening, making free-form spiral shapes that kids love. (I prefer to use a pastry bag fitted with a plain tip, or a heavy-duty plastic bag with a 1/4-inch opening snipped out of one corner to act as a spout.) They are great as a variation on the pancake theme, doused with warm butter and syrup. If you are serving them to a pack of hungry people, use two skillets to speed the frying process.

1 Preheat the oven to 200°F. Line a baking sheet with paper towels. In a large, deep skillet (preferably cast iron), melt shortening over high heat to a depth of 2 to 3 inches and heat it to 375°F.

2 While the shortening is heating, beat the milk and eggs together in a medium bowl. Add the flour, sugar, baking soda, baking powder, and salt and stir until smooth.

3 Transfer half of the batter to a pastry bag fitted with a No. 3 plain tip (1/4 inch wide). To keep the batter from flowing out of the tip, fold over about 2 inches of the tip end of the bag, and hold it against the bag with one hand. Open the top of the bag and pour in the batter with the other hand. Holding the pastry bag over the hot shortening, and moving your hand in tight spirals, let the batter run out of the bag while swirling the batter into a 4- to 6-inch-diame-ter free-form shape. Cook, turning once, until golden brown, about 45 seconds. Using a wire-mesh skimmer, transfer the funnel cake to the paper towels and keep warm in the oven while frying the rest. Separate each new layer of fried funnel cakes with more paper towels. Serve warm, dusted with a sifting of confectioners' sugar, to eat out of hand, or on a plate with melted butter and syrup.

MAKES ABOUT 8 FUNNEL CAKES

Fried Pear Pies

Fried pies have such a melt-in-your-mouth tenderness that many people prefer them to baked pies. In this recipe, lard makes the pastry even more tender. Originally pioneer food, fried pies were cooked in a kettle of fat over a fire, as there were not many ovens on the range.

1 To make the filling: In a large nonstick skillet, heat the butter over medium heat. Add the pears and cook, stirring occasionally, until softened, about 5 minutes. Stir in the sugar, lemon juice, and allspice and continue cooking until the pears are tender, about 3 more minutes. Let cool completely.

2 To make the crust: In a medium bowl, mix the flour and salt. Add the lard or shortening. Using a pastry cutter or 2 knives, cut the lard into the flour until the mixture resembles coarse meal. Tossing with a fork, gradually add the ice water until the mixture is completely moistened and holds together when pressed between your fingers. Gather up the dough, press into a flat disk and wrap in waxed paper. Refrigerate for at least 30 minutes or up to 1 day.

3 Line a baking sheet with waxed paper. On a lightly floured work surface, roll out the dough until 1/8 inch thick. If the dough is well chilled and hard, let it stand at room temperature for a few minutes until softened enough to roll out. Using a 6-inch saucer as a guide, cut out pastry rounds, gathering up the dough scraps and re-rolling as necessary. Place an equal amount of filling on the bottom third of each pastry round. Lightly brush the edges of the rounds with the egg mixture. Fold each round in half to enclose the filling and press the edges sealed with the tines of a fork. Place on the waxed paper and refrigerate while heating the shortening.

4 Place a large wire cake rack over a jelly roll pan. In a deep Dutch oven; melt shortening over high heat to a depth of 2 to 3 inches and heat it to 350°F. In batches, without crowding, deep-fry the pies until golden brown, 4 to 5 minutes. Using a slotted spatula, transfer to the rack to drain. Serve warm or at room temperature.

MAKES 6 PIES

Pear Filling
2 tablespoons unsalted butter
4 firm, ripe Bosc pears, peeled, cored, and cut into 1/2-inch-thick slices
1/3 cup sugar
1 tablespoon fresh lemon juice
1/2 teaspoon ground allspice

Pie Crust
2 cups all-purpose flour
1/2 teaspoon salt
2/3 cup chilled lard or vegetable shortening, cut into 1/2-inch pieces
6 tablespoons ice water

1 large egg yolk beaten with 1 teaspoon water
Vegetable shortening or oil for deep-frying

Bosc pears are firmer than other varieties and don't give off as much juice when cooked. These qualities makes them the best choice for this pie filling.

Sweet Ravioli
with Chocolate-Nut Filling

Chocolate-Nut Filling
½ cup cooked or canned chickpeas, drained
½ cup blanched slivered almonds
4 ounces mixed dried fruit (such as apples, pears, and pitted prunes or apricots), coarsely chopped
3 ounces semisweet chocolate, coarsely chopped
⅓ cup high-quality black currant preserves
½ cup honey
½ cup dark rum

Ravioli Dough
5 cups all-purpose flour
3 tablespoons olive oil
3 tablespoons dry white wine
3 tablespoons water

Vegetable shortening or oil for deep-frying
Confectioners' sugar for dusting

My friend, Manhattan caterer Steve Evasew, shared his family recipe for these ravioli with a difference. The original called for a 5-pound bag of flour, and must make hundreds of dessert ravioli. His family calls them *caginetti*, derived from the Italian word for "chestnut," which the original recipe contained. However, chestnuts were too expensive for poorer families, so they ingeniously substituted chickpeas.

You will need a pasta machine and a couple of days to make this recipe.

1 To make the filling: The day before making the ravioi, put the chickpeas, almonds, dried fruit, and chocolate in a food processor and pulse until processed into a sticky paste. Transfer to a medium bowl and stir in the preserves, honey, and rum. Cover and refrigerate overnight.

2 To make the dough: Put the flour in a food processor. Mix the olive oil, wine, and water in a glass measuring cup. With the machine running, add the liquid through the feed tube and process just until the dough forms a ball on top of the blade. If the dough is too wet or too dry, it will not form a ball. Feel the dough, and if it is sticky and wet, add additional flour, 2 tablespoons at a time, processing after each addition, until the dough forms a ball. If it seems too dry, follow the same procedure, adding additional water, 1 tablespoon at a time. To make the dough by hand, place the flour in a large bowl. Stir in the liquids to make a stiff dough. Turn out onto a lightly floured surface and knead just until smooth, about 5 minutes. Do not overknead the dough. Gather up the dough into a ball, wrap in plastic wrap, and let stand at room temperature for 2 hours.

3 Place a kitchen towel on a baking sheet and dust with flour; set aside. Divide the dough into quarters. Attach a hand-cranked pasta machine to a work surface. Working with 1 portion of dough at a time and keeping the remaining dough covered, fold the dough into thirds and dust with flour on both sides. Pass the dough through the widest setting of the pasta machine (setting No. 1 on most machines). Continue folding and rolling until the dough comes together, usually after 5 or 6 passes. Pass it through a few more times without folding, dusting with flour as needed. Adjust the rollers to the second setting, fold the dough into thirds again, flour both sides, and pass it through the rollers. Continue folding and rolling for 4 or 5 more passes. Adjust the rollers to the third setting, and repeat the folding and rolling for 4 or 5 passes. By now the dough will be transformed into a thin sheet of pasta. Adjust the rollers to the fourth setting. Dust the dough with flour. Without folding, pass the dough through the pasta machine 3 or 4 times. Adjust the rollers to the fifth setting (on most machines, this will be the next-to-last setting). Flour and pass the pasta through the rollers. The dough should be about $\frac{1}{16}$ inch thick.

4 Place the long strip of dough on a work surface. On the bottom half of the dough, about $\frac{1}{2}$ inch from the bottom edge, place scant teaspoons of the filling about $1\frac{1}{2}$ inches apart. Using a pastry brush, lightly brush a border of water around each spoonful of filling. Fold the pasta strip over to cover the filling. Using your fingers, press all around each mound of filling to seal the two layers of pasta together. Using a fluted pastry wheel, cut out $1\frac{1}{2}$-inch-square ravioli. Place the ravioli on the kitchen towel and set aside.

5 Line a baking sheet with paper towels. In a deep Dutch oven, melt vegetable shortening over high heat to a depth of 2 to 3 inches and heat it to 350°F. In batches of about 10, deep-fry the ravioli until golden, about 2 minutes. Using a wire-mesh skimmer, transfer to the paper towels to drain. Let cool completely. (The ravioli can be prepared up to 2 days ahead and stored in an airtight container, with the layers separated with paper towels and waxed paper.) Just before serving, dust the ravioli with the confectioners' sugar.

MAKES ABOUT 5 DOZEN RAVIOLI

Spiced Apple Fritters
with Hard Cider Batter

Vegetable shortening or oil for
  deep-frying

Hard Cider Batter
$2/3$ cup all-purpose flour
$1/8$ teaspoon baking soda
$1/8$ teaspoon salt
$3/4$ cup hard apple cider, preferably
  a medium-dry brand such as
  Bulmer's Woodpecker, or $1/2$ cup
  fruity white wine, such as
  Gewürztraminer, and $1/4$ cup
  apple juice

2 Golden Delicious apples, peeled,
  cored, and cut into 12 wedges
2 tablespoons confectioners' sugar
1 teaspoon Spice Mixture (page 30)

The little town of Occidental, nestled in the California redwoods near Petaluma, is famous for its Italian restaurants, which compete to serve the biggest mountains of delicious family-style dinners. It's been too long since I've been there, but I remember my favorite part of the meal: apple fritters. This is how I make my apple fritters, with light batter scented with hard apple cider and aromatic spices.

1 Preheat the oven to 200°F. Place a large wire cake rack over a jelly roll pan. In a deep Dutch oven, melt vegetable shortening over high heat to a depth of 2 to 3 inches and heat it to 350°F.

2 To make the batter: Sift the flour, baking soda, and salt into a medium bowl. Stir in the cider just until smooth. In batches, dip the apple slices in the batter and place in the hot oil without crowding. Cook until golden brown, about 3 minutes. Using a wire-mesh skimmer, transfer the fritters to the wire rack and keep warm in the oven while frying the rest.

3 In a small bowl, combine the confectioners' sugar and spices. Sift evenly over the fritters and serve immediately.

MAKES 4 SERVINGS

Ricotta Fritters

2 cups (1 pound) ricotta cheese
½ cup all-purpose flour
⅓ cup granulated sugar
2 large eggs
2 tablespoons dark rum
Grated zest of 1 orange
Vegetable shortening or oil for
    deep-frying
Confectioners' sugar for dusting

It's easy recipes like this that give Italian cooking its reputation for delicious, simple food. A few ingredients are stirred together, then transformed into golden puffs to serve for dessert, breakfast, or as a snack with espresso. If you can, make these with freshly made ricotta cheese from an Italian grocer or a cheese shop, and you may find yourself singing an aria or two.

1 If using supermarket ricotta, place the cheese in a paper towel–lined sieve set over a bowl and let stand for 1 hour to drain off excess whey. (Freshly made ricotta is firmer, and doesn't need draining.) Discard the whey and transfer the ricotta to a medium bowl. Stir in the flour, sugar, eggs, rum, and orange zest.

2 Preheat the oven to 200°F. Line a jelly roll pan with crumpled paper towels. In a deep Dutch oven, melt vegetable shortening over high heat to a depth of 2 to 3 inches and heat it to 360°F. In batches, without crowding, carefully drop tablespoonfuls of the batter into the hot oil. Cook, turning once, until golden brown, about 3 minutes. Using a wire-mesh skimmer, transfer to the paper towels and keep warm in the oven while frying the rest of the fritters. Sift the confectioners' sugar over the fritters and serve warm.

MAKES ABOUT 16 FRITTERS

New Orleans Beignets

A trip to New Orleans has many things going for it, but at the top of my list is eating these sweet yeast pastries for breakfast. Because they do not have to rise, beignets are easy to whip up for a special brunch. For the true beignet experience, they should be served with café au lait: coffee (preferably Louisiana style, brewed with ground dried chicory root) combined with a generous amount of boiled milk.

One $\frac{1}{4}$-ounce package active dry
    yeast (2 teaspoons)
$\frac{1}{4}$ cup warm (105° to 115°F) water
3 cups all-purpose flour
$\frac{1}{3}$ cup granulated sugar
$\frac{1}{2}$ teaspoon salt
2 tablespoons chilled vegetable
    shortening
$\frac{1}{2}$ cup evaporated milk
$\frac{1}{3}$ cup water
1 large egg
Vegetable shortening or oil for
    deep-frying
Confectioners' sugar for dusting

1 In a small bowl, sprinkle the yeast over the water and let stand until creamy, about 5 minutes. Stir to dissolve the yeast.

2 In a food processor, pulse the flour, sugar, and salt to combine. Add the shortening and pulse until the mixture is crumbly. In a glass measuring cup, beat the evaporated milk, water, and egg together. With the machine running, add the dissolved yeast and the milk mixture through the feed tube and process until the dough forms a ball on top of the blade. Transfer to a lightly floured work surface and knead briefly, adding more flour if needed, until the dough is soft, but not sticky. To make the dough by hand, mix the flour, sugar, and salt in a large bowl. Add the shortening and cut it into the flour with a pastry blender or 2 knives. Stir in the dissolved yeast and the milk mixture to make a soft dough. Transfer to a lightly floured work surface and knead just until smooth, about 5 minutes. Do not over-knead the dough.

3 Sprinkle the top of the dough with flour and roll out into a 10-by-18-inch rectangle about $\frac{1}{4}$ inch thick. Cut the dough lengthwise into thirds, then crosswise into fifths, to make 15 rectangles. Cover the cut dough with plastic wrap.

4 Preheat the oven to 200°F. Place a large wire cake rack over a jelly roll pan. In a deep Dutch oven, melt shortening over high heat to a depth of 2 to 3 inches and heat it to 360°F. In batches, without crowding, deep-fry the beignets, spooning hot oil over the tops to encourage puffing and turning once, until golden brown, about 3 minutes. Using a wire-mesh skimmer, transfer to the wire rack and keep warm in the oven while frying the rest of the beignets. Let cool slightly and serve warm, with confectioners' sugar sifted over the top.

MAKES 15 BEIGNETS

New Mexican Sopaipillas

2 cups all-purpose flour
2 teaspoons baking powder
½ teaspoon salt
2 tablespoons vegetable shortening,
    plus more for deep-frying
½ cup water
¼ cup milk
¼ cup honey, preferably sage honey
2 teaspoons ground mild chili,
    preferably from Chimayó or Hatch
    chilies, or use regular chili powder
Butter for serving

High altitudes wreak havoc with yeast doughs, so the Native American tribes of the Southwestern high desert make sopaipillas, deep-fried "pillows" of bread leavened with baking powder. Made properly, they are light as a feather, and irresistible when served warm and drizzled with spiced honey. The combination of chilies and honey may seem odd, but you have to try it. In New Mexico, you can buy chili-flavored honey, but it is easy to make your own. If at all possible, use powdered chilies from Chimayó or Hatch, as they are especially sweet-tasting.

1 In a medium bowl, combine the flour, baking powder, and salt. Using a pastry blender or 2 knives, cut the 2 tablespoons shortening into the flour until the mixture resembles coarse meal. Mix in the water and milk to make a soft dough. Gently knead the dough a few times in the bowl just until smooth. Cover the dough with plastic wrap and let stand for 15 minutes.

2 In a small bowl, mix the honey and ground chili. Set aside.

3 Divide the dough in half. On an unfloured work surface, roll out each portion into an 8-inch round. Cut each round into 4 wedges.

4 Preheat the oven to 200°F. Place a wire cake rack in a baking sheet.

5 In a deep Dutch oven, melt shortening to a depth of 2 to 3 inches and heat it to 375°F. In batches, without crowding, deep-fry the sopaipillas, constantly spooning the hot oil over the tops to help them puff, until golden brown, about 3 minutes. Transfer to the cake rack and keep warm in the oven while frying the rest of the sopaipillas. Serve the sopaipillas warm, with the chili-honey and butter.

MAKES 8 SOPAIPILLAS

VARIATION: SUBSTITUTE ½ TEASPOON FRESHLY GROUND ANISEED FOR THE POWDERED CHILI.

Struffoli

1½ cups all-purpose flour
¼ teaspoon salt
3 large eggs at room temperature,
    beaten
1 teaspoon vanilla extract
Vegetable shortening or oil for
    deep-frying
¾ cup honey
2 tablespoons sugar
1 lemon, cut in half
Multi-colored sprinkles for decoration

In many Italian-American households, in the center of all the Christmas sweets you will find struffoli: a mound of tiny fritters glued together with honey and decorated with multi-colored sprinkles. (My friends call it Italian croquembouche, the towering French dessert, which it somewhat resembles, although those puffs are filled and these aren't.) It's the kind of dessert to eat at leisure with a cup of coffee, breaking off bits of the mound with your fingers to nibble as you chat. My thanks to Nancy Verde Barr for her aunt's tip for using the lemon halves to form the mound without burning your fingers on the hot honey.

1 Sift the flour and salt into a medium bowl. Make a well in the center and add the eggs and vanilla. Stir to make a soft dough. Form into a ball, wrap in plastic wrap, and let stand for 30 minutes at room temperature.

2 Line 2 baking sheets with waxed paper. Cut the dough into 6 portions. Keeping the remaining dough covered, on a lightly floured work surface, roll one portion of dough underneath your hands, moving your hands apart in a horizontal movement while rolling, until the dough is rolled and stretched into a long rope about ½ inch wide. Using a sharp knife, cut the dough into ½-inch-long pieces. Place the dough pieces on the waxed paper, separating the pieces so they don't touch. Repeat with the remaining dough, placing half of the dough pieces on each baking sheet. Let stand to slightly dry the dough surfaces, about 15 minutes.

3 Lightly butter a serving platter. Line a roasting pan with crumpled paper towels. In a deep Dutch oven, melt vegetable shortening over high heat to a depth of 2 to 3 inches and heat it to 350°F. Slide the struffoli from 1 sheet of waxed paper into the hot shortening. Deep-fry, stirring occasionally, until golden brown, about 1 minute. Using a wire-mesh skimmer, transfer the dough pieces to the paper towels. Repeat with the remaining dough, separating each new layer of dough with more paper towels.

4 In a saucepan large enough to hold all of the dough pieces, bring the honey and sugar to a boil over high heat, stirring to dissolve the sugar. Boil for 30 seconds. Add all the dough pieces at once and stir gently until covered with the syrup. Pour onto the platter. Using the cut surfaces of the lemon halves, push the dough pieces into a mound, going as high as you can. If the syrup is too hot and liquid and the mound won't hold its shape, wait a few minutes for it to cool, and try again. Decorate with a shower of sprinkles and let cool completely.

Makes 8 to 12 servings

St. Joseph's Zeppole

Rum Filling

1 cup milk

$\frac{1}{3}$ cup granulated sugar

3 large egg yolks

2 tablespoons cornstarch

Pinch of salt

1 tablespoon dark rum

1 teaspoon vanilla extract

Grated zest of $\frac{1}{2}$ orange

$\frac{3}{4}$ cup water

6 tablespoons unsalted butter

1 tablespoon granulated sugar

Grated zest of $\frac{1}{2}$ lemon

$\frac{1}{4}$ teaspoon salt

$\frac{3}{4}$ cup all-purpose flour

$\frac{1}{4}$ teaspoon baking powder

3 large eggs at room temperature

1 teaspoon vanilla extract

Vegetable shortening or oil for
    deep-frying

Thin strips of orange zest or candied
    orange peel for garnish

Confectioners' sugar for dusting

St. Joseph is the patron saint of marital bliss. To celebrate his feast day, Italian housewives make special desserts to keep their husbands happy. No St. Joseph's Day dessert table is complete without zeppole, light-as-a-feather ring-shaped doughnuts with a custard filling. You will need parchment paper and a pastry bag fitted with a fluted tip to shape the zeppole.

1 To make the filling: In a heavy, medium saucepan, bring the milk and sugar to a simmer over medium-low heat, stirring often to dissolve the sugar. Remove from heat. In a small bowl, whisk the egg yolks, cornstarch, and salt together. Gradually whisk the hot milk into the mixture. Rinse out the saucepan and return the mixture to the pan. Stirring constantly with a wooden spatula, bring to a boil over medium-low heat. Remove from heat and stir in the rum, vanilla, and orange zest. Transfer to a small bowl and press plastic wrap directly onto the surface of the custard. Pierce the plastic wrap a few times to allow the steam to escape. Let cool on a wire cake rack until tepid. Refrigerate until chilled, at least 2 hours or overnight.

2 Cut ten 4-inch squares of parchment paper. Using a dark pencil and a small saucer or round cookie cutter as a guide, draw a 3-inch circle on each parchment square. Turn the squares over—you should be able to see the circle through the other side of the paper. In a medium, heavy saucepan, bring the water, butter, sugar, lemon zest, and salt to a boil over medium heat, stirring occasionally so the butter is completely melted by the time the water boils. Add the flour and baking powder and stir until the dough forms a ball that leaves the sides of the pan and begins to film the bottom of the pan, about 1 minute. Remove from heat and let cool for 2 minutes. Stirring constantly, beat in the eggs, one at a time, then the vanilla. Transfer to a pastry bag fitted with a No. 5 fluted open tip (a $\frac{1}{2}$-inch-wide opening). On the pencil-free side of each parchment paper square, piping inside the circle, pipe a 3-inch-wide, $\frac{1}{2}$-inch-thick circle of dough.

3 Place a large wire cake rack over a jelly roll pan. In a deep Dutch oven, melt vegetable shortening over high heat to a depth of 2 to 3 inches and heat it to 375°F. Carefully place a zeppole, on its parchment square, dough-side down in the hot shortening. Add 1 or 2 zeppole to the shortening (or as many as you can without crowding them). Fry until the parchment squares can be lifted off and discarded with kitchen tongs, 20 to 30 seconds. Continue to deep-fry, spooning the hot oil over the zeppole to help them puff and turning them once, about $2\frac{1}{2}$ more minutes. Using a wire-mesh skimmer, transfer to the wire rack to drain. Repeat with the remaining zeppole. Let the zeppole cool completely.

4 Transfer the filling to a clean pastry bag fitted with a No. 5 fluted tip ($\frac{1}{2}$ inch wide). Fill the center hole of each zeppole with a swirl of filling and garnish with a strip of orange zest. If the zeppole have formed properly, the hole won't be too big, and the filling won't fall through when the zeppole are picked up. If the filling threatens to fall through, just pipe a few small rosettes of the filling on the top of each zeppole. Dust the zeppole with the confectioners' sugar. If not serving immediately, cover loosely with plastic wrap and refrigerate for up to 1 day.

MAKES 10 ZEPPOLE

Index

Table of Equivalents

The exact equivalents in the following tables have been rounded for convenience.

Liquid and Dry Measures

U.S.	METRIC
¹/₄ teaspoon	1.25 milliliters
¹/₂ teaspoon	2.5 milliliters
1 teaspoon	5 milliliters
1 tablespoon (3 teaspoons)	15 milliliters
1 fluid ounce (2 tablespoons)	30 milliliters
¹/₄ cup	60 milliliters
¹/₃ cup	80 milliliters
1 cup	240 milliliters
1 pint (2 cups)	480 milliliters
1 quart (4 cups, 32 ounces)	960 milliliters
1 gallon (4 quarts)	3.84 liters
1 ounce (by weight)	28 grams
1 pound	454 grams
2.2 pounds	1 kilogram

Oven Temperatures

FAHRENHEIT	CELSIUS	GAS
250	120	¹/₂
275	140	1
300	150	2
325	160	3
350	180	4
375	190	5
400	200	6
425	220	7
450	230	8
475	240	9
500	260	10

Length Measures

U.S.	METRIC
¹/₈ inch	3 millimeters
¹/₄ inch	6 millimeters
¹/₂ inch	12 millimeters
1 inch	2.5 centimeters